<u>SPECTRE: Shadow of Death</u>

A Critique of Marx' and Engels'
Manifesto of the Communist Party (1848)

By Don Wolfram

Yea, though I walk through the valley of the shadow of death,
I shall fear no evil…Psalm 23:4

Acknowledgments

I try to surround myself with talented people, which makes me appear to be much smarter and more creative than I really am. Now, if they could just make me better looking…

Gene Ort of <u>Gene Michael Productions</u>, the wizard that creates my book covers.

Leah Banicki, for tireless formatting.

My family, for their patience with yet another book.

From a distance in time and space, the voices of a hundred million souls extinguished on this planet by evil men, beckoning to be heard in their collective warning against the Red Plague. I am listening!

Aleksandre Solzhenitsyn, author of *The Gulag Archipelago*, one voice that rose above all others.

<u>**Erratum**</u>

Long ago I learned that the major difference between a hack and a writer is *attention to detail*. The issue is whether the Communist Manifesto (CM) is in the public domain, or whether I would have to get permission from Marx and Engels (or their estates) to reprint CM in part or in its entirety.

An erratum is a publishing device used to correct text or typos after a manuscript is published. Strictly speaking, this is not an erratum, but a correction (I like to say the word "Erratum" because it makes me sound smart). The Latin root means "to stray, or wander". Thus, I wandered away from a proper explanation of public domain, and I am hereby straying back onto the narrow path of *write*-eousness.

Amazon CreateSpace suspended me from publishing *SPECTRE* until I clarified the issue, and they were correct to do so. Here is the skinny on Public Domain (PD) and CM. In the U.S., if a document was published outside of our country a long time ago (I have read both prior to 1900, or more than 70 years prior to the current date) then it is probably in PD.

CM was written and first published in 1848, in the German language. It was translated into English in 1888, by Engels and Samuel Moore (d. 1895). By any calculation, the first English translation is at least 130 years old, and the original pre-dates that by 40 years. There have been other translators, and other printed versions. Based on that, I feel confident in reproducing the entire CM for SPECTRE. Should you be interested, you can follow this URL to the excellent Marxist online library:

<u>https://www.marxists.org/archive/marx/works/1848/communist-manifesto/index.htm</u>

DEDICATION

On Valentine's Day, 2018 a psychopath named Nikolas Cruz shot numerous students and teachers at a school in Parkland, FL in a murderous rampage that left seventeen people dead. The predictable response from the Leftists in the American press corps was to immediately blame the NRA for the horrific killings, even though the NRA had nothing to do with it!

Rather, the NRA promotes responsible firearm safety and legal ownership of weapons. They are staunch defenders not only of the Second Amendment, but of the US Constitution and the American ideal and way of life. I am therefore re-joining the NRA to stand in solidarity with their just cause.

This book is dedicated to those Americans who are not ashamed of their birthright, and who believe that the world is better and safer with our nation strong, under God, indivisible. We must fight to keep ourselves free and to shine the light of liberty around the globe.

And ye shall know the truth, and the truth shall make you free.
John 8:32

Table of contents

Forward 6

Introduction 9

Part I: Manifesto of the Communist Party 14

Part II: Critique of The Communist Manifesto 62

Final words 93

Forward

Communism is a scourge on the earth, a festering sore on the face of humanity, a Red Plague bent on eradicating entire populations based solely on the whims of politics, race, ethnicity, religion, or for no reason other than such a population exists.

Communism did not originate with Karl Marx. It is a political platform vomited from the vilest depths of the blackest souls of humanity. Many other evil societies have come and gone, and will continue to do so as long as people seek to rule over each other. Communism is unique in that it was the first such ideology to come of age when it could be advanced globally.

For most of my fifty seven years I have been studying Communism. When I was a little kid my family lived in the Texas panhandle near a B-52 SAC base. Neighbors were building fallout shelters in their back yards. We could see the vapor trails of fleets of bombers in formation. The Berlin wall, Cuban missile crisis, and Soviet Gulag system were emblematic, scary, and real.

The wall fell, the missile crisis was averted, and the Gulag has been exposed. Even so, Communism is alive, well, and expanding again. North Korea is a greater threat today than ever before, the Russians are again annexing their neighbors, and Venezuela is as Marxist as is Cuba.

Communists, Socialists, Leftists, Progressives (call them what you want, they are all cut from the same filthy cloth) have infiltrated societies the world over. They have been subverting Western culture to create rot and havoc from the inside. America is being threatened from within, and most of the country doesn't even know it.

Call me a conspiracy theorist if you want. That is usually an insult, but what if the conspiracies are real? America has been the greatest global resistance to Communism, and the reason is clear: Communism enslaves people; America sets them free.

Yes, you can argue that America is founded on slavery, that we have exploited the world for our own benefit, on and on *ad nauseam*. Those arguments may need to be debated, but not here. Far more important is that the US Constitution provided a framework to emancipate people not just in America, but globally. This is not to say that we should be in the business of forcing a democratic republic on the rest of the world. Rather, America serves as an enduring example of what can be accomplished when people are set free.

I am an American, and proud of it! Sadly, many of my fellow Americans hate this country, and they have been educated to believe that we are illegitimate and should be beat down and auctioned off to the rest of the world. Thus you see NFL players (and many others) biting the hand that feeds them by ignoring the national anthem and our flag that flies over the graves of millions who have given their lives so that those players can behave like the spoiled brats that they are. Denouncing our Constitution may be guarded by some Amendment, but is nonetheless a disgrace. *I* will never be ashamed of my birthright, despite its dark secrets and imperfections.

SPECTRE is the first in a series, <u>Communism in America,</u> designed to educate my children and other Americans to the growing threat of Communism at home and abroad.

I have no public standing, no fame, no deep pockets to promote this work. Any success will depend on whether readers have an appetite for it and will be willing to carry the fight to their own families, schools, and workplaces. My greatest hope is to openly, publicly debate our American heritage and the great freedoms of our Constitution. If that happens, then I can say I have stuck a finger in the eye of a communist with the war cry:

LET FREEDOM RING!

Introduction

Nineteenth Century Europe was in turmoil. The ancient monarchies were crumbling. Exploration and colonization had led to extreme riches and extreme poverty, supported by an intolerable slave trade. The Industrial Revolution had made magnificent strides in the steel and textiles markets. Business was conducted on a global scale unimaginable to prior generations.

Steam engines and electricity were miraculous scientific tools that were changing the way people worked and the speed at which they moved. Until then, the fastest a human could have travelled was limited to the horse and the sail. By the mid to late 1800s with railroads, steam ships, and soon a Transatlantic Cable, the rate of change must have been staggering. War, the ever-lurking European pastime, would be more and more likely to engulf the entire planet.

Cities were swarmed with peasants seeking work in the huge factories. There were few laws to define workers' rights. Women and children often worked alongside men in the factories and mines. Sanitation and health were virtually ignored, and for many, life was an appalling and desperate existence relieved only by death.

Meanwhile, there was an undercurrent of dissatisfaction amongst the workers. There were real threats of strikes and riots, which were effectively suppressed by authorities, often brutally. (In the early 1800s a faction of British wool weavers revolted against the use of machinery to produce wool cloth in factories; these "Luddites" broke machinery and shut down factories. Parliament responded by making such actions a capital crime, and 14 Luddites were tried and hanged in 1814.)

There were also intellectual critics, writers, and agitators who authored philosophical books and pamphlets. Some formed militant organizations. Many originated in Germany. Two of those intellectuals were Karl Marx and Friedrich Engels. They were determined to change the world. Unfortunately, the only method of change they could conceive was one of total destruction and repudiation of traditional thought, behavior, and social norms. They used new and strange terminology such as *bourgeois*, *proletariat*, *class struggle*, and *Communism*. They wrote prodigiously on politics, economics, and revolution.

Marx' and Engels' crowning achievement was, of course, the *Manifesto of the Communist Party* ("*Manifesto*"). Published originally in 1888, the book (really more a pamphlet than a book) has been immensely successful in defining an ideology and motivating violent revolution around the globe.

Marx (d. 1883) and Engels (d. 1895) did not live long enough to see the fruit of their labor. I have often thought of that, and wondered whether they would have been proud of their accomplishments. Would they rest easily in eternity, knowing that they were to a great extent responsible for the savage genocide of at least 100,000,000 human beings, the vast majority of whom were peasants, workers, and other innocent proletarians? Would they smile at the mention of the names Vladimir Lenin, Joseph Stalin, Mao

Zedong, Ho Chi Minh, Pol Pot, Fidel Castro, Che Guevara, and Kim Jong-un?

Sadly, Communism is still very much alive, and hundreds of millions of people live under its dark cloud to this day. As I write this, North Korea is developing short- and long-range missiles capable of reaching the shores of Japan and the US. Should they proceed much further, it will inevitably lead to war. Even if nuclear holocaust is avoided, the loss of life will be appalling (the vast majority of dead will be millions of North Korean peasants, workers, and other innocent proletarians). Kim Jong-un is only one in a long list of sadistic, narcissistic, megalomaniacal, genocidal Communist dictators.

The purpose of this critique is to give a line-by-line analysis of *Manifesto*. I make every effort at historical accuracy and to confine opinion within that context. All commentary and opinions are mine, for which I ask no pardon. I freely admit that I approach this project with prejudice against Communism. That is my disclaimer. Nonetheless, objectivity is the goal. I encourage the reader to be ruthless in criticism and relentless in pursuit of the truth.

There are many editions of *Manifesto*. Originally published in 1848 in German, the first English translation was not available until 1888. I bought two print copies of *Manifesto* (one a paperback from 1955, the other a hardback from 2010) and a recorded version on CD, which I listen to in my car.

There are many communist websites, some of which are exhaustive and well organized. My favorite is Marxist Internet Archive (www.marxists.org). Though we do not share political values, I greatly appreciate their passion and thoroughness. Much of my research originates there.

I have taken numerous versions of *Manifesto* WORD and PDF documents and compiled them in a neat and readable format with numbered lines (the numbers refer to my original compiled manuscript). I will refer to those numbers to make it easier for cross reference.

Part I thus is *Manifesto*; **Part II** the critique. I recommend reading straight through Part I, then refer back to it as you read Part II. Scribble, make notes, highlight, redline – whatever it takes to understand the text of *Manifesto*, as it is truly important as an historical document.

Critiquing *Manifesto* is ruthless and unforgiving work. You, the student and reader, should be no less so. You may agree or disagree with my conclusions, but do not leave this study without an opinion!

<u>**In the pages of *Manifesto*:**</u>

There is no love, only hate.

There is no peace, only violence.

There is no humility, only arrogance.

There is no joyful music, only tortured screams.

There is no freedom, only chains and slavery.

There is no mercy, only cruelty.

There are few truths, and many lies.

There is nothing sacred; everything is profaned.

The ultimate goal of Communism is world domination, where a very small, elite class of ruthless dictators have control over all nations and peoples, using unimaginable cruelty and suffering to keep themselves in power. Communists have no intention whatsoever of emancipating the proletariat, nor are mercy, justice, or fairness part of any Communist plan.
Communists do NOT share!

[1]Part I: Manifesto of the Communist Party

[5]
by Karl Marx and Frederick Engels

February 1848

Manifesto of the Communist Party

A spectre is haunting Europe – the spectre of communism. All [10]the powers of old Europe have entered into a holy alliance to exorcise this spectre: Pope and Tsar, Metternich and Guizot, French Radicals and German police-spies.

Where is the party in opposition that has not been decried as communistic by its opponents in power? Where is the opposition [15]that has not hurled back the branding reproach of communism, against the more advanced opposition parties, as well as against its reactionary adversaries?

Two things result from this fact:

[20]I. Communism is already acknowledged by all European powers to be itself a power.

II. It is high time that Communists should openly, in the face of the whole world, publish their views, their aims, their tendencies, and meet this nursery tale of the Spectre of Communism with a [25]manifesto of the party itself.

To this end, Communists of various nationalities have assembled in London and sketched the following manifesto, to be published in the English, French, German, Italian, Flemish and Danish languages.

I. Bourgeois and Proletarians

The history of all hitherto existing society is the history of class struggles. Freeman and slave, patrician and plebeian, lord and serf, guild-master and journeyman, in a word, oppressor and [35]oppressed, stood in constant opposition to one another, carried on an uninterrupted, now hidden, now open fight, a fight that each time ended, either in a revolutionary reconstitution of society at large, or in the common ruin of the contending classes.

In the earlier epochs of history, we find almost [40]everywhere a complicated arrangement of society into various orders, a manifold gradation of social rank. In ancient Rome we have patricians, knights, plebeians, slaves; in the Middle Ages, feudal lords, vassals, guild-masters, journeymen, apprentices, serfs; in almost all of these classes, again, subordinate gradations. [45]The modern bourgeois society that has sprouted from the ruins of feudal society has not done away with class antagonisms. It has but established new classes, new conditions of oppression, new forms of struggle in place of the old ones.

Our epoch, the epoch of the bourgeoisie, possesses, [50]however, this distinct feature: it has simplified class antagonisms. Society as a whole is more and more splitting up into two great hostile camps, into two great classes directly facing each other – Bourgeoisie and Proletariat. From the serfs of the Middle Ages sprang the chartered burghers of the earliest towns. [55]From these burgesses the first elements of the bourgeoisie were developed.

The discovery of America, the rounding of the Cape, opened up fresh ground for the rising bourgeoisie. The East-Indian and Chinese markets, the colonization of America, trade [60]with the colonies, the increase in the means of exchange and in commodities generally, gave to commerce, to navigation, to industry, an impulse never before known, and thereby, to the revolutionary element in the tottering feudal society, a rapid development.

[65]   The feudal system of industry, in which industrial production was monopolized by closed guilds, now no longer sufficed for the growing wants of the new markets. The manufacturing system took its place. The guild-masters were pushed on one side by the manufacturing middle class; division [70]of labor between the different corporate guilds vanished in the face of division of labor in each single workshop.

Meantime the markets kept ever growing, the demand ever rising. Even manufacturer no longer sufficed. Thereupon, steam and machinery revolutionized industrial production. The [75]place of manufacture was taken by the giant, Modern Industry; the place of the industrial middle class by industrial millionaires, the leaders of the whole industrial armies, the modern bourgeois.

Modern industry has established the world market, for which the discovery of America paved the way. This market has [80]given an immense development to commerce, to navigation, to communication by land. This development has, in its turn, reacted on the extension of industry; and in proportion as industry, commerce, navigation, railways extended, in the same proportion the bourgeoisie developed, increased its capital, and [85]pushed into the background every class handed down from the Middle Ages.

We see, therefore, how the modern bourgeoisie is itself the product of a long course of development, of a series of revolutions in the modes of production and of exchange. Each [90]step in the development of the bourgeoisie was accompanied by a corresponding political advance of that class. An oppressed class under the sway of the feudal nobility, an armed and self-governing association in the medieval commune: here independent urban republic (as in Italy and Germany); there [95]taxable "third estate" of the monarchy (as in France); afterwards, in the period of manufacturing proper, serving either the semi-feudal or the absolute monarchy as a counterpoise against the nobility, and, in fact, cornerstone of the great monarchies in general, the bourgeoisie has at last, since the [100]establishment of Modern Industry and of the world market, conquered for itself, in the modern representative State, exclusive political sway. The executive of the modern state is but a committee for managing the common affairs of the whole bourgeoisie.

[105] The bourgeoisie, historically, has played a most revolutionary part. The bourgeoisie, wherever it has got the upper hand, has put an end to all feudal, patriarchal, idyllic relations. It has pitilessly torn asunder the motley feudal ties that bound man to his "natural superiors", and has left remaining no other nexus [110]between man and man than naked self-interest, than callous "cash payment". It has drowned the most heavenly ecstasies of religious fervor, of chivalrous enthusiasm, of philistine sentimentalism, in the icy water of

egotistical calculation. It has resolved personal worth into exchange value, and in place of the [115]numberless indefeasible chartered freedoms, has set up that single, unconscionable freedom – Free Trade. In one word, for exploitation, veiled by religious and political illusions, it has substituted naked, shameless, direct, brutal exploitation.

The bourgeoisie has stripped of its halo every occupation [120]hitherto honored and looked up to with reverent awe. It has converted the physician, the lawyer, the priest, the poet, the man of science, into its paid wage labourers.

The bourgeoisie has torn away from the family its sentimental veil, and has reduced the family relation to a mere [125]money relation.

The bourgeoisie has disclosed how it came to pass that the brutal display of vigour in the Middle Ages, which reactionaries so much admire, found its fitting complement in the most slothful indolence. It has been the first to show what man's [130]activity can bring about. It has accomplished wonders far surpassing Egyptian pyramids, Roman aqueducts, and Gothic cathedrals; it has conducted expeditions that put in the shade all former Exoduses of nations and crusades.

The bourgeoisie cannot exist without constantly [135]revolutionizing the instruments of production, and thereby the relations of production, and with them the whole relations of society. Conservation of the old modes of production in unaltered form, was, on the contrary, the first condition of existence for all earlier industrial classes. Constant revolutionizing of production, [140]uninterrupted disturbance of all social conditions, everlasting uncertainty and agitation distinguish the bourgeois epoch from all earlier ones. All fixed, fast-frozen relations, with their train of ancient and venerable prejudices and opinions, are swept away, all new-formed ones become antiquated before they can ossify. [145]All that is solid melts into air, all that is holy is profaned, and man is at last compelled to face with sober senses his real conditions of life, and his relations with his kind.

The need of a constantly expanding market for its products chases the bourgeoisie over the entire surface of the [150]globe. It must nestle everywhere, settle everywhere, establish connections everywhere. The bourgeoisie has through its exploitation of the world market given a cosmopolitan character to production and consumption in every country. To the great chagrin of Reactionists, it has drawn from under the feet of [155]industry the national ground on which it stood. All old-established national industries have been destroyed or are daily being destroyed. They are dislodged by new industries, whose introduction becomes a life and death question for all civilized nations, by industries that no longer work up indigenous raw [160]material, but raw material drawn from the remotest zones; industries whose products are consumed, not only at home, but in every quarter of the globe. In place of the old wants, satisfied by the production of the country, we find new wants, requiring for their satisfaction the products of distant lands and climes. In [165]place of the old local and national seclusion and self-sufficiency, we have intercourse in every direction, universal inter-dependence of nations.

And as in material, so also in intellectual production. The intellectual creations of individual nations become common property. National one-sidedness and [170]narrow-mindedness become more and more impossible, and from the numerous national and local literatures, there arises a world literature.

The bourgeoisie, by the rapid improvement of all instruments of production, by the immensely facilitated means of [175]communication, draws all, even the most barbarian, nations into civilization. The cheap prices of commodities are the heavy artillery with which it batters down all Chinese walls, with which it forces the barbarians' intensely obstinate hatred of foreigners to capitulate. It compels all nations, on pain of extinction, to [180]adopt the bourgeois mode of production; it compels them to introduce what it calls civilization into their midst, i.e., to become bourgeois themselves. In one word, it creates a world after its own image.

The bourgeoisie has subjected the country to the rule of [185]the towns. It has created enormous cities, has greatly increased the urban population as compared with the rural, and has thus rescued a considerable part of the population from the idiocy of rural life. Just as it has made the country dependent on the towns, so it has made barbarian and semi-barbarian countries dependent [190]on the civilized ones, nations of peasants on nations of bourgeois, the East on the West.

The bourgeoisie keeps more and more doing away with the scattered state of the population, of the means of production, and of property. It has agglomerated population, centralized the [195]means of production, and has concentrated property in a few hands. The necessary consequence of this was political centralization. Independent, or but loosely connected provinces, with separate interests, laws, governments, and systems of taxation, became lumped together into one nation, with one [200]government, one code of laws, one national class-interest, one frontier, and one customs-tariff.

The bourgeoisie, during its rule of scarce one hundred years, has created more massive and more colossal productive forces than have all preceding generations together. Subjection [205]of Nature's forces to man, machinery, application of chemistry to industry and agriculture, steam-navigation, railways, electric telegraphs, clearing of whole continents for cultivation, canalization of rivers, whole populations conjured out of the ground – what earlier century had even a presentiment that such [210]productive forces slumbered in the lap of social labor?

We see then: the means of production and of exchange, on whose foundation the bourgeoisie built itself up, were generated in feudal society. At a certain stage in the development of these means of production and of exchange, the conditions [215]under which feudal society produced and exchanged, the feudal organization of agriculture and manufacturing industry, in one word, the feudal relations of property became no longer compatible with the already developed productive forces; they became so many fetters. They had to be burst asunder; they were [220]burst asunder.

Into their place stepped free competition, accompanied by a social and political constitution adapted in it, and the economic and political sway of the bourgeois class.

A similar movement is going on before our own eyes. [225]Modern bourgeois society, with its relations of production, of exchange and of property, a society that has conjured up such gigantic means of production and of exchange, is like the sorcerer who is no longer able to control the powers of the nether world whom he has called up by his spells. For many a decade past the [230]history of industry and commerce is but the history of the revolt of modern productive forces against modern conditions of production, against the property relations that are the conditions for the existence of the bourgeois and of its rule. It is enough to mention the commercial crises that by their periodical return put [235]the existence of the entire bourgeois society on its trial, each time more threateningly. In these crises, a great part not only of the existing products, but also of the previously created productive forces, are periodically destroyed. In these crises, there breaks out an epidemic that, in all earlier epochs, would [240]have seemed an absurdity – the epidemic of over-production. Society suddenly finds itself put back into a state of momentary barbarism; it appears as if a famine, a universal war of devastation, had cut off the supply of every means of subsistence; industry and commerce seem to be destroyed; and why? Because [245]there is too much civilization, too much means of subsistence, too much industry, too much commerce. The productive forces at the disposal of society no longer tend to further the development of the conditions of bourgeois property; on the contrary, they have become too powerful for these conditions, by [250]which they are fettered, and so soon as they overcome these fetters, they bring disorder into the whole of bourgeois society, endanger the existence of bourgeois property. The conditions of bourgeois society are too narrow to comprise the wealth created by them. And how does the bourgeoisie get over these crises? On [255]the one hand by enforced destruction of a mass of productive forces; on the other, by the conquest of new markets, and by the more thorough exploitation of the old ones. That is to say, by paving the way for more extensive and more destructive crises, and by diminishing the means whereby crises are prevented.

[260]   The weapons with which the bourgeoisie felled feudalism to the ground are now turned against the bourgeoisie itself. But not only has the bourgeoisie forged the weapons that bring death to itself; it has also called into existence the men who are to wield those weapons – the modern working class – the proletarians.

[265]   In proportion as the bourgeoisie, i.e., capital, is developed, in the same proportion is the proletariat, the modern working class, developed – a class of laborers, who live only so long as they find work, and who find work only so long as their labor increases capital. These laborers, who must sell themselves [270]piecemeal, are a commodity, like every other article of commerce, and are consequently exposed to all the vicissitudes of competition, to all the fluctuations of the market.

Owing to the extensive use of machinery, and to the division of labor, the work of the proletarians has lost all individual [275]character, and, consequently, all charm for the workman. He becomes an appendage of the machine, and it is only the most simple, most monotonous, and most easily acquired knack, that is required of him. Hence, the cost of production of a workman is restricted, almost entirely, to the means of subsistence that he [280]requires for maintenance, and for the propagation of his race. But the price of a commodity, and therefore also of labor, is equal to its cost of production. In proportion, therefore, as the repulsiveness of the work increases, the wage decreases. Nay more, in proportion as the use of machinery and division of labor [285]increases, in the same proportion the burden of toil also increases, whether by prolongation of the working hours, by the increase of the work exacted in a given time or by increased speed of machinery, etc.

Modern Industry has converted the little workshop of the [290]patriarchal master into the great factory of the industrial capitalist. Masses of labourers, crowded into the factory, are organized like soldiers. As privates of the industrial army they are placed under the command of a perfect hierarchy of officers and sergeants. Not only are they slaves of the bourgeois class, [295]and of the bourgeois State; they are daily and hourly enslaved by the machine, by the overlooker, and, above all, by the individual bourgeois manufacturer himself. The more openly this despotism proclaims gain to be its end and aim, the more petty, the more hateful and the more embittering it is.

[300]   The less the skill and exertion of strength implied in manual labor, in other words, the more modern industry becomes developed, the more is the labor of men superseded by that of women.

Differences of age and sex have no longer any distinctive social validity for the working class. All are instruments of labor, [305]more or less expensive to use, according to their age and sex.

No sooner is the exploitation of the laborer by the manufacturer, so far, at an end, that he receives his wages in cash, than he is set upon by the other portions of the bourgeoisie, the landlord, the shopkeeper, the pawnbroker, etc.

[310] The lower strata of the middle class – the small tradespeople, shopkeepers, and retired tradesmen generally, the handicraftsmen and peasants – all these sink gradually into the proletariat, partly because their diminutive capital does not suffice for the scale on which Modern Industry is carried on, and [315]is swamped in the competition with the large capitalists, partly because their specialized skill is rendered worthless by new methods of production. Thus the proletariat is recruited from all classes of the population.

The proletariat goes through various stages of [320]development. With its birth begins its struggle with the bourgeoisie. At first the contest is carried on by individual labourers, then by the workpeople of a factory, then by the operative of one trade, in one locality, against the individual bourgeois who directly exploits them. They direct their attacks [325]not against the bourgeois conditions of production, but against the instruments of production themselves; they destroy imported wares that compete with their labor, they smash to pieces machinery, they set factories ablaze, they seek to restore by force the vanished status of the workman of the Middle Ages.

³³⁰ At this stage, the labourers still form an incoherent mass scattered over the whole country, and broken up by their mutual competition. If anywhere they unite to form more compact bodies, this is not yet the consequence of their own active union, but of the union of the bourgeoisie, which class, in order to attain [335]its own political ends, is compelled to set the whole proletariat in motion, and is moreover yet, for a time, able to do so. At this stage, therefore, the proletarians do not fight their enemies, but the enemies of their enemies, the remnants of absolute monarchy, the landowners, the non-industrial bourgeois, the petty [340]bourgeois. Thus, the whole historical movement is concentrated in the hands of the bourgeoisie; every victory so obtained is a victory for the bourgeoisie.

But with the development of industry, the proletariat not only increases in number; it becomes concentrated in greater [345]masses, its strength grows, and it feels that strength more. The various interests and conditions of life within the ranks of the proletariat are more and more equalized, in proportion as machinery obliterates all distinctions of labor, and nearly everywhere reduces wages to the same low level. The growing [350]competition among the bourgeois, and the resulting commercial crises, make the wages of the workers ever more fluctuating. The increasing improvement of machinery, ever more rapidly developing, makes their livelihood more and more precarious; the collisions between individual workmen and [355]individual bourgeois take more and more the character of collisions between two classes. Thereupon, the workers begin to form combinations (Trades' Unions) against the bourgeois; they club together in order to keep up the rate of wages; they found permanent associations in order to make provision beforehand [360]for these occasional revolts. Here and there, the contest breaks out into riots.

Now and then the workers are victorious, but only for a time. The real fruit of their battles lies, not in the immediate result, but in the ever expanding union of the workers. This union [365]is helped on by the improved means of communication that are created by modern industry, and that place the workers of different localities in contact with one another. It was just this contact that was needed to centralize the numerous local struggles, all of the same character, into one national struggle [370]between classes. But every class struggle is a political struggle. And that union, to attain which the burghers of the Middle Ages, with their miserable highways, required centuries, the modern proletarian, thanks to railways, achieve in a few years.

[375] This organization of the proletarians into a class, and, consequently into a political party, is continually being upset again by the competition between the workers themselves. But it ever rises up again, stronger, firmer, mightier. It compels legislative recognition of particular interests of the workers, by [380]taking advantage of the divisions among the bourgeoisie itself. Thus, the ten-hours' bill in England was carried.

Altogether collisions between the classes of the old society further, in many ways, the course of development of the proletariat. The bourgeoisie finds itself involved in a constant [385]battle. At first with the aristocracy; later on, with those portions of the bourgeoisie itself, whose interests have become antagonistic to the progress of industry; at all time with the bourgeoisie of foreign countries. In all these battles, it sees itself compelled to appeal to the proletariat, to ask for help, and thus, [390]to drag it into the political arena. The bourgeoisie itself, therefore, supplies the proletariat with its own elements of political and general education, in other words, it furnishes the proletariat with weapons for fighting the bourgeoisie.

Further, as we have already seen, entire sections of the [395]ruling class are, by the advance of industry, precipitated into the proletariat, or are at least threatened in their conditions of existence. These also supply the proletariat with fresh elements of enlightenment and progress.

Finally, in times when the class struggle nears the [400]decisive hour, the progress of dissolution going on within the ruling class, in fact within the whole range of old society, assumes such a violent, glaring character, that a small section of the ruling class cuts itself adrift, and joins the revolutionary class, the class that holds the future in its hands. Just as, therefore, at an [405]earlier period, a section of the nobility went over to the bourgeoisie, so now a portion of the bourgeoisie goes over to the proletariat, and in particular, a portion of the bourgeois ideologists, who have raised themselves to the level of comprehending theoretically the historical movement as a whole.

[410]Of all the classes that stand face to face with the bourgeoisie today, the proletariat alone is a really revolutionary class. The other classes decay and finally disappear in the face of Modern Industry; the proletariat is its special and essential product.

The lower middle class, the small manufacturer, the [415]shopkeeper, the artisan, the peasant, all these fight against the bourgeoisie, to save from extinction their existence as fractions of the middle class. They are therefore not revolutionary, but conservative. Nay more, they are reactionary, for they try to roll back the wheel of history. If by chance, they are revolutionary, [420]they are only so in view of their impending transfer into the proletariat; they thus defend not their present, but their future interests, they desert their own standpoint to place themselves at that of the proletariat.

The "dangerous class", [lumpenproletariat] the social [425]scum, that passively rotting mass thrown off by the lowest layers of the old society, may, here and there, be swept into the movement by a proletarian revolution; its conditions of life, however, prepare it far more for the part of a bribed tool of reactionary intrigue.

[430] In the condition of the proletariat, those of old society at large are already virtually swamped. The proletarian is without property; his relation to his wife and children has no longer anything in common with the bourgeois family relations; modern industry labor, modern subjection to capital, the same in England [435]as in France, in America as in Germany, has stripped him of every trace of national character. Law, morality, religion, are to him so many bourgeois prejudices, behind which lurk in ambush just as many bourgeois interests.

All the preceding classes that got the upper hand sought [440]to fortify their already acquired status by subjecting society at large to their conditions of appropriation. The proletarians cannot become masters of the productive forces of society, except by abolishing their own previous mode of appropriation, and thereby also every other previous mode of appropriation. They have [445]nothing of their own to secure and to fortify; their mission is to destroy all previous securities for, and insurances of, individual property.

All previous historical movements were movements of minorities, or in the interest of minorities. The proletarian [450]movement is the self-conscious, independent movement of the immense majority, in the interest of the immense majority. The proletariat, the lowest stratum of our present society, cannot stir, cannot raise itself up, without the whole superincumbent strata of official society being sprung into the air.

[455]   Though not in substance, yet in form, the struggle of the proletariat with the bourgeoisie is at first a national struggle. The proletariat of each country must, of course, first of all settle matters with its own bourgeoisie. In depicting the most general phases of the development of the proletariat, we traced the more [460]or less veiled civil war, raging within existing society, up to the point where that war breaks out into open revolution, and where the violent overthrow of the bourgeoisie lays the foundation for the sway of the proletariat.

Hitherto, every form of society has been based, as we [465]have already seen, on the antagonism of oppressing and oppressed classes. But in order to oppress a class, certain conditions must be assured to it under which it can, at least, continue its slavish existence. The serf, in the period of serfdom, raised himself to membership in the commune, just as the petty [470]bourgeois, under the yoke of the feudal absolutism, managed to develop into a bourgeois. The modern laborer, on the contrary, instead of rising with the process of industry, sinks deeper and deeper below the conditions of existence of his own class. He becomes a pauper, and pauperism develops more rapidly than [475]population and wealth. And here it becomes evident, that the bourgeoisie is unfit any longer to be the ruling class in society, and to impose its conditions of existence upon society as an over-riding law. It is unfit to rule because it is incompetent to assure an existence to its slave within his slavery, because it cannot help [480]letting him sink into such a state, that it has to feed him, instead of being fed by him. Society can no longer live under this bourgeoisie, in other words, its existence is no longer compatible with society.

The essential conditions for the existence and for the sway of [485]the bourgeois class is the formation and augmentation of capital; the condition for capital is wage-labor. Wage-labor rests exclusively on competition between the labourers. The advance of industry, whose involuntary promoter is the bourgeoisie, replaces the isolation of the labourers, due to competition, by the [490]revolutionary combination, due to association. The development of Modern Industry, therefore, cuts from under its feet the very foundation on which the bourgeoisie produces and appropriates products. What the bourgeoisie therefore produces, above all, are its own grave-diggers. Its fall and the victory of the [495]proletariat are equally inevitable.

II. Proletarians and Communists

In what relation do the Communists stand to the proletarians as a [500]whole? The Communists do not form a separate party opposed to the other working-class parties. They have no interests separate and apart from those of the proletariat as a whole. They do not set up any sectarian principles of their own, by which to shape and mold the proletarian movement.

[505] The Communists are distinguished from the other working-class parties by this only:

1. In the national struggles of the proletarians of the different countries, they point out and bring to the front the common interests of the entire proletariat, independently of all [510]nationality.

2. In the various stages of development which the struggle of the working class against the bourgeoisie has to pass through, they always and everywhere represent the interests of the movement as a whole.

[515] The Communists, therefore, are on the one hand, practically, the most advanced and resolute section of the working-class parties of every country, that section which pushes forward all others; on the other hand, theoretically, they have over the great mass of the proletariat the advantage of clearly [520]understanding the line of march, the conditions, and the ultimate general results of the proletarian movement.

The immediate aim of the Communists is the same as that of all other proletarian parties: formation of the proletariat into a class, overthrow of the bourgeois supremacy, conquest of [525]political power by the proletariat.

The theoretical conclusions of the Communists are in no way based on ideas or principles that have been invented, or discovered, by this or that would-be universal reformer.

They merely express, in general terms, actual relations springing [530]from an existing class struggle, from a historical movement going on under our very eyes. The abolition of existing property relations is not at all a distinctive feature of communism.

All property relations in the past have continually been subject to historical change consequent upon the change in [535]historical conditions. The French Revolution, for example, abolished feudal property in favor of bourgeois property.

The distinguishing feature of Communism is not the abolition of property generally, but the abolition of bourgeois property. But modern bourgeois private property is the final and [540]most complete expression of the system of producing and appropriating products, that is based on class antagonisms, on the exploitation of the many by the few.

In this sense, the theory of the Communists may be summed [545]in the single sentence:

Abolition of private property.

We Communists have been reproached with the desire of abolishing the right of personally acquiring property as the fruit [550]of a man's own labor, which property is alleged to be the groundwork of all personal freedom, activity and independence.

Hard-won, self-acquired, self-earned property! Do you mean the property of petty artisan and of the small peasant, a form of property that preceded the bourgeois form? There is no need to [555]abolish that; the development of industry has to a great extent already destroyed it, and is still destroying it daily.

Or do you mean the modern bourgeois private property?

But does wage-labor create any property for the laborer? Not a bit. It creates capital, i.e., that kind of property which [560]exploits wage-labor, and which cannot increase except upon condition of begetting a new supply of wage-labor for fresh exploitation. Property, in its present form, is based on the antagonism of capital and wage-labor. Let us examine both sides of this antagonism.

[565]To be a capitalist, is to have not only a purely personal, but a social status in production. Capital is a collective product, and only by the united action of many members, nay, in the last resort, only by the united action of all members of society, can it be set in motion.

[570] Capital is therefore not only personal; it is a social power.

When, therefore, capital is converted into common property, into the property of all members of society, personal property is not thereby transformed into social property. It is only the social character of the property that is changed. It loses its [575]class character.

Let us now take wage-labor.

The average price of wage-labor is the minimum wage, i.e., that quantum of the means of subsistence which is absolutely requisite to keep the laborer in bare existence as a laborer. What, [580]therefore, the wage-laborer appropriates by means of his labor, merely suffices to prolong and reproduce a bare existence. We by no means intend to abolish this personal appropriation of the products of labor, an appropriation that is made for the maintenance and reproduction of human life, and that leaves no [585]surplus wherewith to command the labor of others. All that we want to do away with is the miserable character of this appropriation, under which the laborer lives merely to increase capital, and is allowed to live only in so far as the interest of the ruling class requires it.

[590]   In bourgeois society, living labor is but a means to increase accumulated labor. In Communist society, accumulated labor is but a means to widen, to enrich, to promote the existence of the laborer.

In bourgeois society, therefore, the past dominates the [595]present; in Communist society, the present dominates the past. In bourgeois society capital is independent and has individuality, while the living person is dependent and has no individuality.

And the abolition of this state of things is called by the bourgeois, abolition of individuality and freedom! And rightly [600]so. The abolition of bourgeois individuality, bourgeois independence, and bourgeois freedom is undoubtedly aimed at.

By freedom is meant, under the present bourgeois conditions of production, free trade, free selling and buying.

But if selling and buying disappears, free selling and [605]buying disappears also. This talk about free selling and buying, and all the other "brave words" of our bourgeois about freedom in general, have a meaning, if any, only in contrast with restricted selling and buying, with the fettered traders of the Middle Ages, but have no meaning when opposed to the [610]Communistic abolition of buying and selling, of the bourgeois conditions of production, and of the bourgeoisie itself.

You are horrified at our intending to do away with private property. But in your existing society, private property is already done away with for nine-tenths of the population; its existence [615]for the few is solely due to its non-existence in the hands of those nine-tenths. You reproach us, therefore, with intending to do away with a form of property, the necessary condition for whose existence is the non-existence of any property for the immense majority of society.

[620] In one word, you reproach us with intending to do away with your property. Precisely so; that is just what we intend.

From the moment when labor can no longer be converted into capital, money, or rent, into a social power capable of being monopolized, i.e., from the moment when individual property [625]can no longer be transformed into bourgeois property, into capital, from that moment, you say, individuality vanishes.

You must, therefore, confess that by "individual" you mean no other person than the bourgeois, than the middle-class owner of property. This person must, indeed, be swept out of the [630]way, and made impossible.

Communism deprives no man of the power to appropriate the products of society; all that it does is to deprive him of the power to subjugate the labor of others by means of such appropriations.

[635] It has been objected that upon the abolition of private property, all work will cease, and universal laziness will overtake us.

According to this, bourgeois society ought long ago to have gone to the dogs through sheer idleness; for those of its [640]members who work, acquire nothing, and those who acquire anything do not work. The whole of this objection is but another expression of the tautology: that there can no longer be any wage-labor when there is no longer any capital.

All objections urged against the Communistic mode of [645]producing and appropriating material products, have, in the same way, been urged against the Communistic mode of producing and appropriating intellectual products. Just as, to the bourgeois, the disappearance of class property is the disappearance of production itself, so the disappearance of class [650]culture is to him identical with the disappearance of all culture.

That culture, the loss of which he laments, is, for the enormous majority, a mere training to act as a machine.

But don't wrangle with us so long as you apply, to our intended abolition of bourgeois property, the standard of your [655]bourgeois notions of freedom, culture, law, &c. Your very ideas are but the outgrowth of the conditions of your bourgeois production and bourgeois property, just as your jurisprudence is but the will of your class made into a law for all, a will whose essential character and direction are determined by the [660]economical conditions of existence of your class.

The selfish misconception that induces you to transform into eternal laws of nature and of reason, the social forms springing from your present mode of production and form of property – historical relations that rise and disappear in the [665]progress of production – this misconception you share with every ruling class that has preceded you. What you see clearly in the case of ancient property, what you admit in the case of feudal property, you are of course forbidden to admit in the case of your own bourgeois form of property.

[670] Abolition [Aufhebung] of the family! Even the most radical flare up at this infamous proposal of the Communists.

On what foundation is the present family, the bourgeois family, based? On capital, on private gain. In its completely developed form, this family exists only among the bourgeoisie. [675]But this state of things finds its complement in the practical absence of the family among the proletarians, and in public prostitution.

The bourgeois family will vanish as a matter of course when its complement vanishes, and both will vanish with the [680]vanishing of capital.

Do you charge us with wanting to stop the exploitation of children by their parents? To this crime we plead guilty.

But, you say, we destroy the most hallowed of relations, when we replace home education by social.

[685] And your education! Is not that also social, and determined by the social conditions under which you educate, by the intervention direct or indirect, of society, by means of schools, &c.? The Communists have not invented the intervention of society in education; they do but seek to alter the [690]character of that intervention, and to rescue education from the influence of the ruling class.

The bourgeois clap-trap about the family and education, about the hallowed co-relation of parents and child, becomes all the more disgusting, the more, by the action of Modern Industry, [695]all the family ties among the proletarians are torn asunder, and their children transformed into simple articles of commerce and instruments of labor.

But you Communists would introduce community of women, screams the bourgeoisie in chorus.

[700] The bourgeois sees his wife a mere instrument of production. He hears that the instruments of production are to be exploited in common, and, naturally, can come to no other conclusion that the lot of being common to all will likewise fall to the women.

[705] He has not even a suspicion that the real point aimed at is to do away with the status of women as mere instruments of production.

For the rest, nothing is more ridiculous than the virtuous indignation of our bourgeois at the community of women which, [710]they pretend, is to be openly and officially established by the Communists. The Communists have no need to introduce community of women; it has existed almost from time immemorial.

Our bourgeois, not content with having wives and [715]daughters of their proletarians at their disposal, not to speak of common prostitutes, take the greatest pleasure in seducing each other's wives.

Bourgeois marriage is, in reality, a system of wives in common and thus, at the most, what the Communists might [720]possibly be reproached with is that they desire to introduce, in substitution for a hypocritically concealed, an openly legalized community of women. For the rest, it is self-evident that the abolition of the present system of production must bring with it the abolition of the community of women springing from that [725]system, i.e., of prostitution both public and private.

The Communists are further reproached with desiring to abolish countries and nationality.
The working men have no country. We cannot take from them what they have not got. Since the proletariat must first of all [730]acquire political supremacy, must rise to be the leading class of the nation, must constitute itself the nation, it is so far, itself national, though not in the bourgeois sense of the word.

National differences and antagonism between peoples are daily more and more vanishing, owing to the development of the [735]bourgeoisie, to freedom of commerce, to the world market, to uniformity in the mode of production and in the conditions of life corresponding thereto.

The supremacy of the proletariat will cause them to vanish still faster. United action, of the leading civilized countries [740]at least, is one of the first conditions for the emancipation of the proletariat.

In proportion as the exploitation of one individual by another will also be put an end to, the exploitation of one nation by another will also be put an end to. In proportion as the [745]antagonism between classes within the nation vanishes, the hostility of one nation to another will come to an end.

The charges against Communism made from a religious, a philosophical and, generally, from an ideological standpoint, are not deserving of serious examination.

[750] Does it require deep intuition to comprehend that man's ideas, views, and conception, in one word, man's consciousness, changes with every change in the conditions of his material existence, in his social relations and in his social life?

What else does the history of ideas prove, than that [755]intellectual production changes its character in proportion as material production is changed? The ruling ideas of each age have ever been the ideas of its ruling class.

When people speak of the ideas that revolutionize society, they do but express that fact that within the old society the [760]elements of a new one have been created, and that the dissolution of the old ideas keeps even pace with the dissolution of the old conditions of existence.

When the ancient world was in its last throes, the ancient religions were overcome by Christianity. When Christian ideas [765]succumbed in the 18th century to rationalist ideas, feudal society fought its death battle with the then revolutionary bourgeoisie. The ideas of religious liberty and freedom of conscience merely gave expression to the sway of free competition within the domain of knowledge.

[770] "Undoubtedly," it will be said, "religious, moral, philosophical, and juridical ideas have been modified in the course of

historical development. But religion, morality, philosophy, political science, and law, constantly survived this change."

⁷⁷⁵ "There are, besides, eternal truths, such as Freedom, Justice, etc., that are common to all states of society. But Communism abolishes eternal truths, it abolishes all religion, and all morality, instead of constituting them on a new basis; it therefore acts in contradiction to all past historical experience."

⁷⁸⁰ What does this accusation reduce itself to? The history of all past society has consisted in the development of class antagonisms, antagonisms that assumed different forms at different epochs.

But whatever form they may have taken, one fact is ⁷⁸⁵common to all past ages, viz., the exploitation of one part of society by the other. No wonder, then, that the social consciousness of past ages, despite all the multiplicity and variety it displays, moves within certain common forms, or general ideas, which cannot completely vanish except with the total ⁷⁹⁰disappearance of class antagonisms.

The Communist revolution is the most radical rupture with traditional property relations; no wonder that its development involved the most radical rupture with traditional ideas.

⁷⁹⁵But let us have done with the bourgeois objections to Communism.

We have seen above, that the first step in the revolution by the working class is to raise the proletariat to the position of ruling class to win the battle of democracy.

⁸⁰⁰ The proletariat will use its political supremacy to wrest, by degree, all capital from the bourgeoisie, to centralize all instruments of production in the hands of the State, i.e., of the proletariat

organized as the ruling class; and to increase the total productive forces as rapidly as possible.

[805] Of course, in the beginning, this cannot be effected except by means of despotic inroads on the rights of property, and on the conditions of bourgeois production; by means of measures, therefore, which appear economically insufficient and untenable, but which, in the course of the movement, outstrip themselves, [810]necessitate further inroads upon the old social order, and are unavoidable as a means of entirely revolutionizing the mode of production.

These measures will, of course, be different in different countries. Nevertheless, in most advanced countries, the [815]following will be pretty generally applicable.

1. Abolition of property in land and application of all rents of land to public purposes.

2. A heavy progressive or graduated income tax.

[820]3. Abolition of all rights of inheritance.

4. Confiscation of the property of all emigrants and rebels.

5. Centralization of credit in the hands of the State, by means of a national bank with State capital and an exclusive monopoly.

6. Centralization of the means of communication and transport in [825]the hands of the State.

7. Extension of factories and instruments of production owned by the State; the bringing into cultivation of waste-lands, and the improvement of the soil generally in accordance with a common plan.

[830]8. Equal liability of all to work. Establishment of industrial armies, especially for agriculture.

9. Combination of agriculture with manufacturing industries; gradual abolition of all the distinction between town and country by a more equable distribution of the populace over the country.

[835]10. Free education for all children in public schools. Abolition of children's factory labor in its present form. Combination of education with industrial production, &c, &c.

When, in the course of development, class distinctions [840]have disappeared, and all production has been concentrated in the hands of a vast association of the whole nation, the public power will lose its political character. Political power, properly so called, is merely the organized power of one class for oppressing another. If the proletariat during its contest with the [845]bourgeoisie is compelled, by the force of circumstances, to organize itself as a class, if, by means of a revolution, it makes itself the ruling class, and, as such, sweeps away by force the old conditions of production, then it will, along with these conditions, have swept away the conditions for the existence of [850]class antagonisms and of classes generally, and will thereby have abolished its own supremacy as a class.

In place of the old bourgeois society, with its classes and class antagonisms, we shall have an association, in which the free development of each is the condition for the free development of [855]all.

III. Socialist and Communist Literature

[860]1. Reactionary Socialism

A. Feudal Socialism

Owing to their historical position, it became the vocation of the aristocracies of France and England to write pamphlets against modern bourgeois society. In the French Revolution of [865]July 1830, and in the English reform agitation, these aristocracies again succumbed to the hateful upstart. Thenceforth, a serious political struggle was altogether out of the question. A literary battle alone remained possible. But even in the domain of literature the old cries of the restoration period had [870]become impossible.

In order to arouse sympathy, the aristocracy was obliged to lose sight, apparently, of its own interests, and to formulate their indictment against the bourgeoisie in the interest of the exploited working class alone. Thus, the aristocracy took their [875]revenge by singing lampoons on their new masters and whispering in his ears sinister prophesies of coming catastrophe.

In this way arose feudal Socialism: half lamentation, half lampoon; half an echo of the past, half menace of the future; at times, by its bitter, witty and incisive criticism, striking the [880]bourgeoisie to the very heart's core; but always ludicrous in its effect, through total incapacity to comprehend the march of modern history.

The aristocracy, in order to rally the people to them, waved the proletarian alms-bag in front for a banner. But the [885]people, so often as it joined them, saw on their hindquarters the old feudal coats of arms, and deserted with loud and irreverent laughter.

One section of the French Legitimists and "Young England" exhibited this spectacle. In pointing out that their mode [890]of exploitation was different to that of the bourgeoisie, the feudalists forget that they exploited under circumstances and conditions that were quite different and that are now antiquated. In showing that, under their rule, the modern proletariat never existed, they forget that the modern bourgeoisie is the necessary [895]offspring of their own form of society.

For the rest, so little do they conceal the reactionary character of their criticism that their chief accusation against the bourgeois amounts to this, that under the bourgeois régime a class is being developed which is destined to cut up root and branch [900]the old order of society.

What they upbraid the bourgeoisie with is not so much that it creates a proletariat as that it creates a revolutionary proletariat.
In political practice, therefore, they join in all coercive measures [905]against the working class; and in ordinary life, despite their high-falutin phrases, they stoop to pick up the golden apples dropped from the tree of industry, and to barter truth, love, and honor, for traffic in wool, beetroot-sugar, and potato spirits.

As the parson has ever gone hand in hand with the [910]landlord, so has Clerical Socialism with Feudal Socialism.

Nothing is easier than to give Christian asceticism a Socialist tinge. Has not Christianity declaimed against private property, against marriage, against the State? Has it not preached in the place of these, charity and poverty, celibacy and [915]mortification of the flesh, monastic life and Mother Church? Christian Socialism is but the holy water with which the priest consecrates the heart-burnings of the aristocrat.

B. Petty-Bourgeois Socialism

[920]The feudal aristocracy was not the only class that was ruined by the bourgeoisie, not the only class whose conditions of existence pined and perished in the atmosphere of modern bourgeois society. The medieval burgesses and the small peasant proprietors were the precursors of the modern bourgeoisie. In [925]those countries which are but little developed, industrially and commercially, these two classes still vegetate side by side with the rising bourgeoisie.

In countries where modern civilization has become fully developed, a new class of petty bourgeois has been formed, [930]fluctuating between proletariat and bourgeoisie, and ever renewing itself as a supplementary part of bourgeois society. The individual members of this class, however, are being constantly hurled down into the proletariat by the action of competition, and, as modern industry develops, they even see the moment [935]approaching when they will completely disappear as an independent section of modern society, to be replaced in manufactures, agriculture and commerce, by overlookers, bailiffs and shopmen.

In countries like France, where the peasants constitute far [940]more than half of the population, it was natural that writers who sided with the proletariat against the bourgeoisie should use, in their criticism of the bourgeois régime, the standard of the peasant and petty bourgeois, and from the standpoint of these intermediate classes, should take up the cudgels for the working [945]class. Thus arose petty-bourgeois Socialism. Sismondi was the head of this school, not only in France but also in England.

This school of Socialism dissected with great acuteness the contradictions in the conditions of modern production. It laid bare the hypocritical apologies of economists. It proved, [950]incontrovertibly, the disastrous effects of machinery and division of labor; the concentration of capital and land in a few hands; overproduction and crises; it pointed out the inevitable ruin of the petty bourgeois and peasant, the misery of the proletariat, the anarchy in production, the crying inequalities in [955]the distribution of wealth, the industrial war of extermination between nations, the dissolution of old moral bonds, of the old family relations, of the old nationalities.

In its positive aims, however, this form of Socialism aspires either to restoring the old means of production and of [960]exchange, and with them the old property relations, and the old society, or to cramping the modern means of production and of exchange within the framework of the old property relations that have been, and were bound to be, exploded by those means. In either case, it is both reactionary and Utopian.

[965] Its last words are: corporate guilds for manufacture; patriarchal relations in agriculture.

Ultimately, when stubborn historical facts had dispersed all intoxicating effects of self-deception, this form of Socialism ended in a miserable fit of the blues.

970

C. German or "True" Socialism

The Socialist and Communist literature of France, a literature that originated under the pressure of a bourgeoisie in power, and that was the expression of the struggle against this power, was [975]introduced into Germany at a time when the bourgeoisie, in that country, had just begun its contest with feudal absolutism.

German philosophers, would-be philosophers, and beaux esprits (men of letters), eagerly seized on this literature, only forgetting, that when these writings immigrated from France into [980]Germany, French social conditions had not immigrated along with them. In contact with German social conditions, this French literature lost all its immediate practical significance and assumed a purely literary aspect. Thus, to the German philosophers of the Eighteenth Century, the demands of the first [985]French Revolution were nothing more than the demands of "Practical Reason" in general, and the utterance of the will of the revolutionary French bourgeoisie signified, in their eyes, the laws of pure Will, of Will as it was bound to be, of true human Will generally.

[990]   The work of the German literati consisted solely in bringing the new French ideas into harmony with their ancient philosophical conscience, or rather, in annexing the French ideas without deserting their own philosophic point of view.

This annexation took place in the same way in which a [995]foreign language is appropriated, namely, by translation.

It is well known how the monks wrote silly lives of Catholic Saints over the manuscripts on which the classical works of ancient heathendom had been written. The German literati reversed this process with the profane French literature. [1000]They wrote their philosophical nonsense beneath the French original. For instance, beneath the French criticism of the economic functions of money, they wrote "Alienation of Humanity", and beneath the French criticism of the bourgeois state they wrote "Dethronement of the Category of the General", [1005]and so forth.

The introduction of these philosophical phrases at the back of the French historical criticisms, they dubbed "Philosophy of Action", "True Socialism", "German Science of Socialism", "Philosophical Foundation of Socialism", and so on.

[1010] The French Socialist and Communist literature was thus completely emasculated. And, since it ceased in the hands of the German to express the struggle of one class with the other, he felt conscious of having overcome "French one-sidedness" and of representing, not true requirements, but the requirements of [1015]Truth; not the interests of the proletariat, but the interests of Human Nature, of Man in general, who belongs to no class, has no reality, who exists only in the misty realm of philosophical fantasy.

This German socialism, which took its schoolboy task so [1020]seriously and solemnly, and extolled its poor stock-in-trade in such a mountebank fashion, meanwhile gradually lost its pedantic innocence.

The fight of the Germans, and especially of the Prussian bourgeoisie, against feudal aristocracy and absolute monarchy, [1025] in other words, the liberal movement, became more earnest. By this, the long-wished for opportunity was offered to "True" Socialism of confronting the political movement with the Socialist demands, of hurling the traditional anathemas against liberalism, against representative government, against bourgeois [1030] competition, bourgeois freedom of the press, bourgeois legislation, bourgeois liberty and equality, and of preaching to the masses that they had nothing to gain, and everything to lose, by this bourgeois movement. German Socialism forgot, in the nick of time, that the French criticism, whose silly echo it was, [1035] presupposed the existence of modern bourgeois society, with its corresponding economic conditions of existence, and the political constitution adapted thereto, the very things whose attainment was the object of the pending struggle in Germany.

To the absolute governments, with their following of [1040] parsons, professors, country squires, and officials, it served as a welcome scarecrow against the threatening bourgeoisie.

It was a sweet finish, after the bitter pills of flogging and bullets, with which these same governments, just at that time, dosed the German working-class risings.

[1045] While this "True" Socialism thus served the government as a weapon for fighting the German bourgeoisie, it, at the same time, directly represented a reactionary interest, the interest of German Philistines. In Germany, the petty-bourgeois class, a relic of the sixteenth century, and since then constantly cropping [1050]up again under the various forms, is the real social basis of the existing state of things.

To preserve this class is to preserve the existing state of things in Germany. The industrial and political supremacy of the bourgeoisie threatens it with certain destruction – on the one [1055]hand, from the concentration of capital; on the other, from the rise of a revolutionary proletariat. "True" Socialism appeared to kill these two birds with one stone. It spread like an epidemic.

The robe of speculative cobwebs, embroidered with flowers of rhetoric, steeped in the dew of sickly sentiment, this [1060]transcendental robe in which the German Socialists wrapped their sorry "eternal truths", all skin and bone, served to wonderfully increase the sale of their goods amongst such a public.

And on its part German Socialism recognized, more and [1065]more, its own calling as the bombastic representative of the petty-bourgeois Philistine.

It proclaimed the German nation to be the model nation, and the German petty Philistine to be the typical man. To every villainous meanness of this model man, it gave a hidden, higher, [1070]Socialistic interpretation, the exact contrary of its real character. It went to the extreme length of directly opposing the "brutally destructive" tendency of Communism, and of proclaiming its supreme and impartial contempt of all class struggles. With very few exceptions, all the so-called Socialist [1075]and Communist publications that now (1847) circulate in Germany belong to the domain of this foul and enervating literature.

[1080]2. Conservative or Bourgeois Socialism

A part of the bourgeoisie is desirous of redressing social grievances in order to secure the continued existence of bourgeois society.

To this section belong economists, philanthropists, [1085]humanitarians, improvers of the condition of the working class, organizers of charity, members of societies for the prevention of cruelty to animals, temperance fanatics, hole-and-corner reformers of every imaginable kind. This form of socialism has, moreover, been worked out into complete systems.

[1090] We may cite Proudhon's Philosophie de la Misère as an example of this form.

The Socialistic bourgeois want all the advantages of modern social conditions without the struggles and dangers necessarily resulting therefrom. They desire the existing state of [1095]society, minus its revolutionary and disintegrating elements. They wish for a bourgeoisie without a proletariat. The bourgeoisie naturally conceives the world in which it is supreme to be the best; and bourgeois Socialism develops this comfortable conception into various more or less complete systems. In [1100]requiring the proletariat to carry out such a system, and thereby to march straightway into the social New Jerusalem, it but requires in reality, that the proletariat should remain within the bounds of existing society, but should cast away all its hateful ideas concerning the bourgeoisie.

1105   A second, and more practical, but less systematic, form of this Socialism sought to depreciate every revolutionary movement in the eyes of the working class by showing that no mere political reform, but only a change in the material conditions of existence, in economical relations, could be of any 1110advantage to them. By changes in the material conditions of existence, this form of Socialism, however, by no means understands abolition of the bourgeois relations of production, an abolition that can be affected only by a revolution, but administrative reforms, based on the continued existence of these 1115relations; reforms, therefore, that in no respect affect the relations between capital and labor, but, at the best, lessen the cost, and simplify the administrative work, of bourgeois government.

Bourgeois Socialism attains adequate expression when, 1120and only when, it becomes a mere figure of speech.

Free trade: for the benefit of the working class. Protective duties: for the benefit of the working class. Prison Reform: for the benefit of the working class. This is the last word and the only seriously meant word of bourgeois socialism.

1125   It is summed up in the phrase: the bourgeois is a bourgeois –
for the benefit of the working class.

3. Critical-Utopian Socialism and Communism

We do not here refer to that literature which, in every great [1130]modern revolution, has always given voice to the demands of the proletariat, such as the writings of Babeuf and others.

The first direct attempts of the proletariat to attain its own ends, made in times of universal excitement, when feudal society was being overthrown, necessarily failed, owing to the then [1135]undeveloped state of the proletariat, as well as to the absence of the economic conditions for its emancipation, conditions that had yet to be produced, and could be produced by the impending bourgeois epoch alone. The revolutionary literature that accompanied these first movements of the proletariat had [1140]necessarily a reactionary character. It inculcated universal asceticism and social levelling in its crudest form.

The Socialist and Communist systems, properly so called, those of Saint-Simon, Fourier, Owen, and others, spring into existence in the early undeveloped period, described above, of [1145]the struggle between proletariat and bourgeoisie (see Section I. Bourgeois and Proletarians).

The founders of these systems see, indeed, the class antagonisms, as well as the action of the decomposing elements in the prevailing form of society. But the proletariat, as yet in its [1150]infancy, offers to them the spectacle of a class without any historical initiative or any independent political movement.

Since the development of class antagonism keeps even pace with the development of industry, the economic situation, as they find it, does not as yet offer to them the material [1155]conditions for the emancipation of the proletariat. They therefore search after a new social science, after new social laws, that are to create these conditions.

Historical action is to yield to their personal inventive action; historically created conditions of emancipation to [1160]fantastic ones; and the gradual, spontaneous class organization of the proletariat to an organization of society especially contrived by these inventors. Future history resolves itself, in their eyes, into the propaganda and the practical carrying out of their social plans.

[1165]In the formation of their plans, they are conscious of caring chiefly for the interests of the working class, as being the most suffering class. Only from the point of view of being the most suffering class does the proletariat exist for them.

The undeveloped state of the class struggle, as well as [1170]their own surroundings, causes Socialists of this kind to consider themselves far superior to all class antagonisms. They want to improve the condition of every member of society, even that of the most favored. Hence, they habitually appeal to society at large, without the distinction of class; nay, by preference, to [1175]the ruling class. For how can people, when once they understand their system, fail to see in it the best possible plan of the best possible state of society?

Hence, they reject all political, and especially all revolutionary action; they wish to attain their ends by peaceful [1180]means, necessarily doomed to failure, and by the force of example, to pave the way for the new social Gospel.

Such fantastic pictures of future society, painted at a time when the proletariat is still in a very undeveloped state and has but a fantastic conception of its own position, correspond with [1185]the first instinctive yearnings of that class for a general reconstruction of society.

But these Socialist and Communist publications contain also a critical element. They attack every principle of existing society. Hence, they are full of the most valuable materials for [1190]the enlightenment of the working class. The practical measures proposed in them – such as the abolition of the distinction between town and country, of the family, of the carrying on of industries for the account of private individuals, and of the wage system, the proclamation of social harmony, the [1195]conversion of the function of the state into a more superintendence of production – all these proposals point solely to the disappearance of class antagonisms which were, at that time, only just cropping up, and which, in these publications, are recognized in their earliest indistinct and undefined forms only. [1200]These proposals, therefore, are of a purely Utopian character.

The significance of Critical-Utopian Socialism and Communism bears an inverse relation to historical development. In proportion as the modern class struggle develops and takes definite shape, this fantastic standing apart from the contest, these

[1205]fantastic attacks on it, lose all practical value and all theoretical justification. Therefore, although the originators of these systems were, in many respects, revolutionary, their disciples have, in every case, formed mere reactionary sects. They hold fast by the original views of their masters, in [1210]opposition to the progressive historical development of the proletariat. They, therefore, endeavor, and that consistently, to deaden the class struggle and to reconcile the class antagonisms. They still dream of experimental realization of their social Utopias, of founding isolated "phalansteres", of establishing [1215]"Home Colonies", or setting up a "Little Icaria" – duodecimo editions of the New Jerusalem – and to realize all these castles in the air, they are compelled to appeal to the feelings and purses of the bourgeois. By degrees, they sink into the category of the reactionary conservative Socialists depicted above, differing [1220]from these only by more systematic pedantry, and by their fanatical and superstitious belief in the miraculous effects of their social science.

They, therefore, violently oppose all political action on the part of the working class; such action, according to them, can [1225]only result from blind unbelief in the new Gospel.

The Owenites in England, and the Fourierists in France, respectively, oppose the Chartists and the Réformistes.

IV. Position of the Communists in Relation to the Various [1230] Existing Opposition Parties

Section II has made clear the relations of the Communists to the existing working-class parties, such as the Chartists in England and the Agrarian Reformers in America.

[1235] The Communists fight for the attainment of the immediate aims, for the enforcement of the momentary interests of the working class; but in the movement of the present, they also represent and take care of the future of that movement. In France, the Communists ally with the Social-Democrats against [1240]the conservative and radical bourgeoisie, reserving, however, the right to take up a critical position in regard to phases and illusions traditionally handed down from the great Revolution.

In Switzerland, they support the Radicals, without losing sight of the fact that this party consists of antagonistic elements, [1245]partly of Democratic Socialists, in the French sense, partly of radical bourgeois.

In Poland, they support the party that insists on an agrarian revolution as the prime condition for national emancipation, that party which fomented the insurrection of [1250]Cracow in 1846.

In Germany, they fight with the bourgeoisie whenever it acts in a revolutionary way, against the absolute monarchy, the feudal squirearchy, and the petty bourgeoisie.

But they never cease, for a single instant, to instill into the [1255]working class the clearest possible recognition of the hostile antagonism between bourgeoisie and proletariat, in order that the German workers may straightway use, as so many weapons against the bourgeoisie, the social and political conditions that the bourgeoisie must necessarily introduce along with its [1260]supremacy, and in order that, after the fall of the reactionary classes in Germany, the fight against the bourgeoisie itself may immediately begin.

The Communists turn their attention chiefly to Germany, because that country is on the eve of a bourgeois revolution that [1265]is bound to be carried out under more advanced conditions of European civilization and with a much more developed proletariat than that of England was in the seventeenth, and France in the eighteenth century, and because the bourgeois revolution in Germany will be but the prelude to an immediately [1270]following proletarian revolution.

In short, the Communists everywhere support every revolutionary movement against the existing social and political order of things.

In all these movements, they bring to the front, as the [1275]leading question in each, the property question, no matter what its degree of development at the time.
Finally, they labor everywhere for the union and agreement of the democratic parties of all countries.

The Communists disdain to conceal their views and aims. [1280]They openly declare that their ends can be attained only by the forcible overthrow of all existing social conditions. Let the ruling classes tremble at a Communistic revolution. The proletarians have nothing to lose but their chains. They have a world to win.
[1285]

Working Men of All Countries, Unite!

Part II: Critique of *The Communist Manifesto*

[8]**Spectre:** *some object or source of terror or dread*

[http://www.dictionary.com/browse/spectre]

Marx chose to open with an allegory that came true. A "spectre" is a dark, foreboding, ghostly, and evil apparition. Communism is indeed the embodiment of a spectre.

[10]**Powers of old Europe:** Marx is wholly committed to the destruction of tradition and authority as the enemies of Communism.

[14-21]By the mid-1800s, Communists were already notorious and reviled by traditional society.

[26-27]Marx met with others in London in 1847 as *The Communist League*. The Manifesto was the product of their rather inauspicious beginnings and met acclaim only later, after Marx' death. Initially published in German, English translations appeared in 1888.

[30]Marx popularized the terms *Bourgeois* (Fr. "Burgher"; ruling class) and *Proletarian* (Latin; poor or working class). In Communist parlance, the Bourgeois are the wealthy, capitalist ruling class that must be swept aside by the Proletariat.

[39]The basic premise of Communism is conflict: the Bourgeois subjugate the Proletariat. This tension leads inevitably to the rise of the Proletariat and the violent overthrow of the Bourgeois. (Interestingly, the US Constitution provides a framework for a harmonious society bound by laws. Communists, in their hatred of humanity, have never reconciled that phenomenon.)

Communist ideology promotes the concept of a classless global society where there will be no need for struggle and all people will work as much as they deem necessary, and each will provide for and take from the common good.

Capitalism has provided for a robust middle class, especially in America. That middle class has provided the opportunity for people to better themselves and rise above poverty.

[57]America has always been the thorn in the side, the fly in the ointment, and the obvious antithesis of Communism. Under American capitalism, a person can be born poor and strive to better himself as he has energy and stamina to persevere.

[87-104]Marx uses one of the most effective tools in the Communist repertoire – creating an enemy, real or imagined, and focusing on that theme. In this case the enemy is social class. The method is class envy and, more importantly, class hatred. The bourgeois represent wealth, political power, and influence. (We will see that the Communists must be THE political party, to the exclusion of all other parties, on pain of torture and death.)

[105-147]This diatribe demonstrates one of the many hypocrisies of Communism. Marx and Engels actually belonged to – and were dependent upon – the bourgeois, very willing to feed at its troughs, lavishing in its largesse, all the while conspiring to bite the hand that feeds. They decry the loss of feudalism and family as if those were revered, yet Communist ideology tears all tradition and societal fabric to shreds in its never-ending quest for dominance and control. Communists feign to overthrow one oppression on behalf of the proletariat, only to replace it with another, far worse oppression.

[148-157]Marx decries the march of capitalism to the far reaches of the globe, yet the stated purpose of Communism is to destroy "the existing social and political order of things"[1271-1273] in a relentless quest for world domination through violent revolution.

[173-183]This is the pot calling the kettle black. Communists (usually a small minority of a nation) force their will upon largely *UN*willing populations on pain of imprisonment, torture, and genocide, to adopt Marxist principles even though it inevitably means social upheaval and self-destruction of the society.

[184-201]Marx again seems to be pining for the old ways. Ironically, the tactic of forced urbanizations was perfected by Stalin in the Five Year Plan and Mao Zedong with the Great Leap Forward. Millions of peasants were moved off their farms onto "collectives" or moved into the cities to work in factories. Both ideas were absurdly unrealistic and ultimately led to economic ruin, unmitigated suffering, and the deaths of tens of millions of peasants, mostly from starvation and slave labor.

[201-264]Early in the Soviet transformation to a fully Communist society, Lenin unleashed the "modern working class".[263-264] Meant, of course, to stick a thumb into the capitalists' eyes, what he discovered instead was his thumb up his own arse. Lenin replaced Marx' fetters of feudalism[219] with the fetters of the Socialist state. The policy failed due to the heavy hand of oppressive taxes[818]. Instead of prosperity and equality, the proletariat again found itself at the bottom of society, and starvation was the price they had to pay.

To Lenin's credit, he realized that Communism was a miserable failure. Unfortunately, his pride demanded that he make excuses for the debacle, so he retreated to rethink his strategy. To buy time he issued the New Economic Policy (NEP). The NEP was very clearly a capitalist answer to a Communist problem: societies work better in a competitive marketplace. Lenin even invited "bourgeois experts" to run the factories, of course under the watchful eyes of the Party.

(For an excellent read on the NEP, see Richard Fleming's *Lenin's Conception of Socialism: Learning from the early experiences of the world's first socialist revolution*)

https://www.marxists.org/history/erol/ncm-7/lenin-socialism.htm

Jeremiah predicted this three millennia before: *...O foolish people, and without understanding; which have eyes and see not; which have ears and hear not...* Jeremiah 5:21.

Marx, Lenin, Stalin, and a host of others in their individual and collective folly are so committed to the Communist ideology that they are willing to continue making the same failed decisions to prove the unprovable. Human nature cannot be changed by mandate, force, writing, or wishful thinking.

Human nature is spiritual. Flawed to be sure, it craves freedom, love, and a unique identity. To think otherwise is arrogance and delusion, yet that is the Communist way. Sadly, millions of innocent peasants and workers are simply grist in the mill of the Marxist experiment, and Communist history is written in their blood. [265-309]The Industrial Revolution did indeed bring great change to the world. Much of the change was inevitable, if you believe in the inevitability of technology and understand the reasons why technology advances relentlessly and creates its own momentum.

Marx shouldn't have hated it so, if it really did so much destruction to tradition and families. He should have been grateful for the head start and the opportunities that it gave to Communists!

From a domestic perspective, the comment on landlords was founded on a despicable truth. Much of Europe at the time had laws that protected absentee landowners, many of whom were very wealthy and owned properties as inherited estates. (In the 1880s James Hott of America toured Europe extensively; he was a keen observer of the human condition, and wrote with great passion on the landlords and poverty in the United Kingdom. See Ch. III of *Journeyings in the Old World, by James W. Hott, D.D., United Brethren Publishing House, 1884).*

Marx' comment on exploitation of women[300-305] is pure hypocrisy. Marx in his private life certainly had no qualms against taking advantage of women of low estate; more on that to follow.

[310-495]This section is lengthy, as it develops the principles of class envy and antagonism.

"Envy" is not an adequate term. I might envy my neighbor's tomato plants or my brother's fishing skills, but I don't conspire to kill them for it. Class envy in a Marxist Communist world is extreme hatred, and it leads inevitably to murder. This is not simply a crime of passion; rather, it is a crime that feeds itself and stops only when the perpetrators die. It is a crime that builds on its own bloodlust like a prairie fire before a south wind consuming everything in its path.

Communism is itself a criminal enterprise that appeals to the lowest strata of society and human nature. The Russian Marxist revolution was funded by the Georgian street thug and bank robber

Joseph Jughashvili Stalin and facilitated by the traitor Vladimir Lenin with the cooperation of German military agents.

[313]Capital (money for investments) and property rights (specifically land and factories) are the recurrent themes of Communist angst. By focusing on those, Marx was able to create the necessary polarization between the established order (monied class, oppressors) and the victims (workers, oppressed). Communism has always thrived on creating and maintaining a strong base of victims to use as a wedge. (21st Century Communists use the same tactics and, true to their ideology, very effectively create new classes of victims even when those victims don't exist.)

In American capitalism, almost anyone can own property or start a business; indeed, workers are encouraged to invest in businesses. Those who learn to do so can take their "diminutive capital" * and turn it into a modest fortune if they are thrifty and hard working.

*In 2018 House Minority Leader Nancy Pelosi insulted the millions of working Americans who received bonuses due to the 2017 Republican tax cuts. She called those bonuses – some in the thousands of dollars or the equivalent in company stock – "crumbs". Mrs. Pelosi's crumb is another's bread…

[336-340]By the end of the 1800s, monarchies were teetering on the edge of oblivion, and they did not heed the calls for social reform. They became the targets of strife, and eventually their royal households were torn down or made irrelevant.

[343-361]Trades' Unions continue to develop. Marx correctly predicted the violent clashes of the workers in protest of working conditions and wages.

The Chicago Haymarket Riot (May 4, 1886)* is a perfect example of the polarizing nature of labor unions. A group of workers were protesting in support of an eight-hour work day. Reports vary; tens of thousands had marched the day before, and on May 4 about 1500 gathered for a scheduled rally. Rain drove most away, and police moved in to disperse the remaining few hundred. A bomb was thrown at the police; shots were fired; in the ensuing chaos, 12 police and protesters were killed, and scores wounded.

*Not surprising, the alleged leaders of the riot were "German-born labor radicals" http://www.history.com/this-day-in-history/the-haymarket-square-riot. The labor union? The Federation of Organized Trades and Labor Unions, the predecessor of the American Federation of Labor (AFL) http://www.illinoislaborhistory.org/the-haymarket-affair/.

[362-393]Labor unions were the key to success*. They became the strike forces, the mobs doing the bidding of the bosses, both bourgeois and proletarian. It is not an intellectual overreach to equate labor unions with police or military arms of political parties; that is exactly how Marx sees them.[375-376]

*In modern America, these mobs are led by community organizers and are not true unions. The 2016 election of Donald Trump exposed the soft underbelly – many unions swung away from the Democrat Party when Hillary Clinton called them "deplorables". I consider myself to be a deplorable, a "blue collar professional". I know many other such deplorables and respect their work, much of which is demanding and dangerous and puts them in harm's way. Makes me wonder, did Mrs. Clinton ever do demanding, dangerous union work that put her in harm's way?

Mob action will occasionally have positive consequences. The *Ten Hours Act, 1847* is an example of improving the workplace, limiting women's and children's workdays to ten hours during the week, and eight hours on Saturdays.[378-381]

Venezuela is a modern example of a country torn asunder by Marxist politics.[381-393] Hugo Chavez was a Communist agitator, elected president in 1998, served in that capacity until his death in 2013 and followed in office by Nicolas Maduro. In true Marxist fashion, Venezuela has been savagely divided by labor unions. Failed government policies have resulted in extreme inflation, driving earning power so low that the country is essentially in poverty. (Ironically, Venezuela sits on what is reported to be the world's greatest oil reserves.)

According to Marx, Venezuela should by now be a well-developed proletarian state. Sadly, for the masses of the population, a Communist ideology has (again) crushed the very lives of the proletariat.

[394-429]Marx continues to develop the theme of violence, the real linchpin of Communism. Forceful, violent coercion is what Communists use to suppress their subjects. It is human nature to dominate and control; Marx plays on that nature, setting one class against another. This is no call to a higher cause, but an appeal to humanity's lowest common denominator.

The *lumpenproletariat*[424] (mobs and useful idiots) is present in every society, and a key factor in any dictator's plans. Ruthless, degenerate, amoral, they exist for momentary satisfaction and the whims of the leaders. The greatest danger, of course, lay in the fact that under Communism, which destroys all rule of law, the most ruthless and cunning rise to power. Joseph Stalin, Mao Zedong, Pol

Pot – all came from or depended upon this dubious clique to perpetuate the Communist way.

(Marx belongs to the intellectual equivalent, the *lumpenfauxintellectualis*,* educated bums. Such today are state-controlled fake journalists, liberal professors, and bureaucrats embedded in government office. They are effectively the propaganda arm of the Communist Party and its many Leftist political affiliates. All they lack is jack boots on the necks of their political opponents.)

*Phrase coined by the author.

Ruthless, degenerate, amoral, Marx existed for the satisfaction of a base ideology. It is doubtful that Marx or Engels ever did manual labor. They would have considered such an endeavor beneath them, because work is fit only for the working class. Communism breeds elitism and class hatred.

[430-447]This section sets the stage for the black heart of Communism. Class hatred; anarchy; treachery; destruction of tradition, law, and the Church; theft of money and crushing of the economy.

The *raison d'etre* is this: Communism is a totalitarian war on freedom, individuality, and private property with the ultimate goal of world domination.

[448-463]The Communist call to arms. Marx in his elitist arrogance deigns to speak for the masses, the workers, the proletariat. The caveat is that true Communists are always in the minority, arriving on the scene as agitators and community organizers, using the thugs and criminal element to do their bidding, to "settle matters with its own bourgeoisie".[457-458]

Communists create or augment existing strife for their nefarious ends. When they say, "…the violent overthrow of the bourgeoisie"[462] they are inciting mob action to engage in anarchy and murder, usually resulting in genocide. Once such civil wars begin, millions of people die, many of them innocent victims, collateral damage, mere slavish pawns on the Communist chess board.

[464-495]To fan the flames of war, Communists divide the population along class lines; those with wealth, education, influence, and property are deemed the oppressors. All others are the oppressed, victims who must be avenged. Since there is no way to get the satisfaction of the avenger through legal means, all law and society must be swept away immediately, catastrophically, causing immense suffering which can then be blamed on the oppressor class.

What follows is relatively easy. Prison, torture, executions all feed the bloodlust of the masses. Once the oppressors are vanquished, the Communist leaders take the spoils for themselves.

In a benevolent society, people are allowed the freedom to become what they are as individuals and as citizens in a greater culture. In America, capitalism provides the opportunity for citizens to aspire to greatness both as individuals and as part of a well-ordered country. Capital is used as a means to create wealth, and is the rising tide that lifts all ships. All workers are encouraged to participate through pension plans, 401k retirement, and individual investments.

On the other hand, Communists are elitists; *they alone* know what is best for a society. Instead of gradually lifting the whole, they swiftly crush it. Once that is accomplished, the Communists step onto the rotting mass of what used to be a society, and *they alone* rise above it. *They alone* have dominion, and the proletarians become their slaves.

497-525Proletarians and Communists. Marx paints a very benign, paternal picture of Communism, as if the proletarians were children and the Communists benevolent schoolmasters looking out for the interests of all. Likewise, the Communists claim to represent all disparate factions of the proletariat, irrespective of country or race. In this the Communists behave much as arbitrators or impartial judges, willing to give each group a place and position. The Communists would simply become *primus inter pares* ("first among equals"), altruistic, wise, caring, empathetic.

Nothing could be further from the truth! Communists dominate everything and everyone. They are the ultimate bullies, making and changing the rules to suit themselves, using terror and murder to gain and keep power. Communists use the proletariat, then throw them on the trash heap. Lenin was a perfect example of this. When his Bolsheviks could not win by the merits of their platform, he simply changed the rules and banished the Mensheviks. Stalin took that much further, eliminating all of his competition (real and perceived) in fits of paranoid slaughter. (Among the tens of millions of Stalin's victims were Army officers, estimated at 20,000 in one purge in the 1930s, murdered and stacked in rows like so much firewood.)

526-542In this section, Marx tries to justify the theft of private property, making the excuse that such theft is not unique to Communists.531-546 In practice, however, it is one of the most important means of revenge against society's business leaders. Lenin, Stalin, and Mao all participated in this, and it always failed to bring the promised universal prosperity. Decades later in Venezuela, Cuba, and Nicaragua this was used to confiscate the factories of international corporations in the name of the State. Not surprisingly, when those economies were wrecked, so were the livelihoods of millions of proletarian families; the vast majority were plunged into poverty. The "victory of the proletariat"[494-495] and their "conquest of political power"[524-525] really meant victory and conquest only for the Communist elite.

[544-575]Marx claims one unifying theme: Abolition of private property. This undoubtedly resonates with those who do not own any property. The Soviet form of property confiscation and redistribution led to a disastrous drop in farm production, followed by waves of famine. Add heavy taxes to the mix and you can see that the proletarians are to be used again at the whim of the State.

Marxist theory would have one believe that *if* bourgeois property is redistributed, *and* all of the capital is "converted into common property",[572] *then* society will lose all of its social stigmas and equality will reign. Society will self-govern, and people will simply participate and take responsibility not only for themselves but for all of society.

There is not a country on earth that has ever behaved in such a way. Let's go back several centuries to North American natives. Before European settlers arrived, there were millions of indigenous people across the continent. They had no capital, no money, no factories, no great cities. Many tribes were nomadic, and they hunted or fished to feed themselves. In Marxist theory, they should have been living happily in an expansive society free from class distinctions.

Nonsense! Native American tribes were extremely class conscious! Their societies were very hierarchical, with chiefs and warriors, and women did most of the daily work and cared for children. Life was hard, and living day to day required extraordinary effort just to survive. Resources were not unlimited, and tribes had territories. There was a perpetual state of war or a high level of threat. Strong tribes subjugated the weak, and slavery or death were the price of defeat in battle.

In Mexico, Central and South America, there were great civilizations that built huge cities, had road systems, and engaged in commerce. They were happy to coexist, and as their societies advanced they lost all class character, just as Marx predicted – right?

Of course not! The Aztec and Mayan cultures were extremely divided. They were ruled by kings, and had extraordinarily complex religions. They protected and expanded their territories through war. The strong subjugated the weak. There was a huge slave trade to build the pyramids, observatories, and palaces for the wealthy classes. Hundreds of thousands were worked to death, or were sacrificed to appease the bloodlust of their gods.

When left to themselves, people divide into classes. They fight, build cities, and engage in commerce. There is a constant state of war or high level of threat. The strong subjugate the weak. This is called "humanity." When humans make rules of behavior, it is called "society".

[576-597]Marx embarks on a diatribe describing wage-labor. He defines minimum wage as the average of all wage labor. It is important to understand that in modern America, minimum wage is a government standard definition. In Marx' time it is very unlikely that European governments set such standards. (Germany did not have an official minimum wage until 2014!) One may criticize Marx for his erroneous math, but his point is well taken: European workers were paid at the lowest wage that the market could bear, and poverty was widespread.

The fault in Marx' star is that Communism will bring a new wave of prosperity and raise the living standards of the common worker. Reality is much different. When Communists take over economies are ruined, resulting in wave after wave of famine due to inept government policies. (Millions of Soviet and Chinese citizens were reduced to starvation, some even turning to cannibalism.)

Marx' 19th Century Communist dream became the 20th Century nightmare. The utopian road was paved over the mass graves of the proletariat.

[598-634]Back to attacks on private property, individuality, and free trade. Marx' obsession with class hatred is reiterated in another call for murder of anyone of means, wealth, capital, property or business ownership. *This person must indeed be swept out of the way, and made impossible.*[626-630] Marx also wants to do away with the marketplace, of buying and selling altogether.[604-611]

Here enters another lesson on human nature. Marx persists in the belief that human beings, if relieved of all class distinctions, will simply get along. Take away all monetary systems, all markets, all capitalists, and people will gravitate towards equality and altruism, and any desire for individuality will melt away.

Unfortunately, the only way to get there is to eliminate anyone and anything that stands in the way. Violence and mass murder were used very effectively by the Soviets, Chinese, Khmer Rouge, and other Communist revolutions. They all purported to be cleansing society for the proletariat. Unfortunately for the proletariat, the perpetrators of such purges were the most vile and vicious members of a new hierarchy, and they held the reins of power. Once that power was attained, there was no desire to share. Communist leaders simply become the new ruling class. Though they would never admit it, they become the new capitalists, the new property owners, the new royalty. They become the new bourgeois, and the proletariat became the slaves.

One of the most striking – indeed, insulting – passages in Manifesto is, *Communism deprives no man of the power to appropriate the products of society; all that it does is to deprive him of the power to subjugate the labor of others by means of such appropriations.* [631-634] This is no misprint, but a lie used to beguile the masses, a promise to give away stuff to those workers who have little, thus enriching their impoverished existence. (This tactic is being used in Venezuela in the 21st Century, to what end? That country is in freefall economic collapse.)

Marx elsewhere stated that "…religion…is the opium of the people." *Religion is the sigh of the oppressed creature, the heart of a heartless world, and the soul of soulless conditions. It is the opium of the people…*

Communists are hardly different; their "opiate" is the promise of free stuff: land, property, health care, education, revenge on the wealthy oppressor classes.

When Marx is corrected by history, the above paragraph should read:

Communism allows no *working man (proletarian) the power to appropriate the products of his own society; all it does is give the Communist elite the power to subjugate the labor of others, to starve and work the proletariat to death, all in the name of a false, evil, corrupt ideology. Communism ultimately is a cult of personality, sacrificing the lives of the proletariat on the altar of greed and power.*

[637-669]Marx is pursuing an intellectual discourse on what must, to him, have been pure fantasy – the concept of work, of physical labor, of getting one's hands dirty. Indeed, had Marx ever done an honest day's labor, he may have had a better appreciation for the proletariat. Marx and his benefactor Engels were of the *lumpenfauxintellectualis*. They obviously profited from others' labors (Marx deigned to speak for them; Engels' family fortunes were made from them).

Marx spent his days in carousing, drinking, and raping the house staff. A notorious drunk, he would from time to time have periods of manic (and maniacal) writing; thus his legacy. One can only imagine what Marx might have become had he been sober and true to his family calling of ministry. If nothing else, had Marx spent his years in honest labor, at least the accusations of hypocrisy would have been somewhat hollow.

[644-647]Here, Marx defends *the Communistic mode of producing and appropriating products.* History demonstrates that the "Communist mode" of appropriating anything is through violence, coercion, and terror. Marx' arrogance is on display when he discusses the bourgeois work ethic. All the factories and machines had to come from somewhere, and people worked hard to create them.

No doubt, at the time Marx would have seen the idle rich, second or third generation playboys spending their fathers' hard-earned cash in frivolity and wanton debauchery. One can speculate to his motives, but keep in mind that Marx depended on the largesse of Engels, a second or third generation playboy spending his father's hard-earned cash! Shakespeare might have misquoted himself:

Methinks the Commie doth protest too much!

This sentiment persists into the 21st Century. As recently as 2012 in America, there was a popular political phrase: *You didn't build that!** Meant as a slur, it became a slogan of Leftists, used to appeal to a naïve voting base who wanted nothing more than to tear down any successful individual or corporation simply because their success represented wealth that they (the modern proletariat) envied.

*Deplorables can check out the reference:

https://www.youtube.com/watch?v=YKjPI6no5ng

This is Communist dogma. In a Socialist world, success is considered a sin. Anyone with wealth and social status are automatically assumed to have arrived there by taking advantage of someone else. Communist agitators ("community organizers") use this lie as a ploy to anger those whose existence is less by any Communist standard. Success is somehow unfair, must necessarily have been obtained by cheating or coercing innocent others, and must therefore be abolished.

Communists are not original; they are simply terrorists. They thrive by aggravating, by agitating, by promising that the unfair gains of a few will be distributed equally to the many. Communists build nothing of enduring value. Rather, they deign to enforce equality by dragging all down to the lowest common denominator. Far better that all should be poor than for a few to have more than their fair share. The capitalist concept that "a rising tide lifts all boats" is anathema.

Marx goes on another tirade against "freedom, culture, and law".[653-669] At the time of the writing of *Manifesto*, Marx was living in England, taking money from his benefactor Engels, and creating a document that, if Marx had his way, would destroy England and all of Europe, and spread its vile revolutionary influence around the world.

The fact that the European bourgeoisie even *had* freedom, culture, and law ate at his dark soul like a cancer. The mere thought that there were people of means, of success, and of social standing was so repulsive that the only recourse to that intolerable situation was to kill them all.

Marx fancied himself to be an astute historian. He realized that European monarchies were falling. In his mind, however, royal heads weren't falling fast enough, and he demanded that Communists pick up the pace and be the vanguard. His arrogance was profound.

Had Marx been an *honest* historian, he would have shown respect for the country that created the Magna Carta; he could have worked with the social reformers of the day. He would have realized that the US Constitution provided a framework for a just society. He would know from his religious upbringing and early faith (abandoned in his twenties) that the teachings of Jesus espoused equality under God, care for the poor, and justice for women and children.

One way to illustrate Marx' attitude toward the bourgeoisie is to think of kids on a playground. The cool kids have more stuff, better clothes, and substantial lunches with store-bought cookies; Marx is wearing hand-me-downs, eats stale bread, and sits alone. He is envious of the cool kids and wants to be part of that clique, but he knows that he will never fit in.

Marx could learn to compete. He could seek out his own group of friends, play his own games, and ignore the cool kids. He could use his intelligence to create something useful to society, or use his family influence to gain status.

These ideas may have had a small foothold in Marx' psyche in his late teens, but at some point he gave himself over to the brooding, dark hater that became his place in history. He had no intention of competing. On the playground of life, the ball wasn't his so he couldn't make the team. He took the path of jealousy and strife, and chose to destroy his enemies, real or imagined. If *he* couldn't play, nobody would play.

[670-725]Here Marx is approaching the core of Communism: control the family and children's education. That, with the abolition of religious freedom, ensures complete domination by the Socialist state. It is hard

to imagine that anything in Marx' upbringing could have been so bad as to justify this diatribe. (Stalin likewise rejected the Church. His mother had wanted him to be a priest.)

He rants and rambles in self-righteous indignation against what he reports as debauchery of the wealthy.[708-725] One would gather from reading Marx that all the bourgeois do is go about town, whoring and carousing, seducing each other's wives, and abusing all the poor children. (Did Marx observe this in Engels' life? Engels shacked with his girlfriend, never married, and would have been a source of insider knowledge into the lifestyles of the rich.) If all of that were true, how then did the bourgeois find the time to build and manage factories?

As for education, one of the basic ten points of Communism is to control the education system.[835-837] History would later demonstrate how effective this was in creating a new society. Stories abound of children being taught to hate their parents in the name of the State, to reveal family secrets even if it meant the death of their parents. If that alone is accomplished, then it would take a mere decade to eradicate a generation of parents and usher in a new generation of children who are brainwashed automatons devoted to Communism.

As it so happened, Marx made himself one of history's great bigots.[708-725] Most of history's Communist leaders took the hint and behaved in like fashion, taking multiple wives and abandoning them as it suited their fancies. Some family members were driven to suicide (Stalin's wife shot herself, or was murdered by Stalin's own hand; his grown son, captured by Germans, was abandoned by Stalin and driven to his death in captivity).

Communism makes its own rules, and the end justifies the means. If Communist leaders truly served their families and the proletarians, then they would be faithful to those respective entities. However, dictators do not attain power by self-sacrifice so much as by sacrificing others. How convenient to have no moral boundary, no spiritual authority, no civil bond! Those in power can give full rein to their sadistic and sexual appetites, and who dares stand against them? [726-769]Marx transitions from destroying family ties to destroying nations; truly, if he can accomplish the former, it is but a logical step to accomplish the latter. Ironically, as Communist dictators develop their evil schemes they will always demand loyalty to the Party above all else – above self, friendship, business, family, faith, and nation. However, Communist revolutionaries are by default traitors to their mother countries. A rational observer *should* ask, "If so-and-so is willing to abandon his faith, family, and nation, why would I expect anything better?"

Marx and Engels were traitors to Germany; Lenin a traitor to Russia; Mao a traitor to China, and on and on, an endless procession of megalomaniacal murderers demanding loyalty from others while demonstrating loyalty, ultimately, only to themselves. How convenient….and a hundred million lives later have changed nothing. A traitor is a traitor, treacherous and sniveling, cowardly, selfish, amoral. (A true patriot, a nationalist, would take the position of fighting for the common good, not caring who gets the glory.)

Marx envisioned a world order, an international Communism. [728-746]"Working men have no country," and, "the supremacy of the proletariat." It is very strange that Marx would write, *national differences and antagonism between peoples are daily more and more vanishing*[733-734] when the entire premise of *Manifesto* is based on class hatred and antagonism. "Fantasy" more accurately describes this passage; Marx did not want antagonisms to vanish, nor does Communism promote any such idea.

Lenin and Stalin clearly demonstrated that "the supremacy of the proletariat will cause them (antagonisms) to vanish still faster"[738] was simply a pretext to increase control over entire nations. Communist leaders lust for power, and have no intention of sharing that power with nations or individuals.

It is important to reiterate and understand this principle:

The ultimate goal of Communism is world domination, where a very small, elite class of ruthless dictators have control over all nations and peoples, using unimaginable cruelty and suffering to keep themselves in power. Communists have no intention whatsoever of emancipating the proletariat, nor are mercy, justice,
or fairness part of any Communist plan.

Communists do NOT *share!*

[747-855]The Ten Commandments of the Communist Manifesto. This is where Marx drives a stake through the heart and soul of humanity, not simply rejecting but destroying the framework of society: law, freedom, justice, faith (particularly Christianity), property, and capital.

Civil society is not based on whim or fancy; it is not based on conscience. Marx is right when he states, "man's consciousness, changes with every change in the conditions of his material existence".[750-753] That is exactly why civil societies have laws to protect freedom, justice, faith, property, and capital!

Communism *is* based on conscience – a broken, seared, dark, amoral conscience that places a dictatorial soul at the center, with all other ideas in orbit around and subject to that dark soul. Those other ideas are compressed and consumed and banished on pain of death, as if they never existed.

Marx makes certain that no other competing ideas are given any consideration: *The charges made against Communism…are not deserving of serious examination.*[747-749] About one hundred years later Mao used a ploy to drive this home. He invited rival leaders to discuss ideologies that opposed his own repressive policies, thus exposing those leaders as enemies of the State and destined for torture and execution.

Marx goes on to relegate Christianity to the trash heap of history.[763-769] He should know – as a young man, Marx was a devout Christian, and wrote beautifully in praise of the Christian faith. Unfortunately, he made a complete turnaround and became an atheist. He would forever after see Christianity as a threat to his own ideas of world dominion.

There is a very good reason why Communists are atheists: religion is a higher authority, and to Communists, there is no authority higher than the Communist state. Ironically, some Communist dictators rise to the level of deities, and surround themselves with cadres of worshipping subjects. In such circumstances they create de facto religions (cults of personality).

Manifesto makes numerous mentions of America. Marx grew up in an era immediately following the American Declaration of Independence. Indeed, America rose up as a nation to throw off the bonds of oppression. Marx should have been thrilled and inspired; alas, he had only spite for the American experiment, because the resulting Constitution gave people freedom and guaranteed that freedom as given by God, the ultimate authority:

We hold these Truths to be self-evident, that all Men

are created equal, that they are endowed by their Creator

with certain unalienable rights, that among these are

Life, Liberty, and the pursuit of Happiness...

(Second paragraph of the Declaration of Independence,

Second Continental Congress, July 4, 1776)

The US Constitution and America became the eternal thorn in the side of Communism. There is a clear line of demarcation between the two with one leading to freedom, the other to chains and slavery: *...Communism abolishes eternal truths, it abolishes all religion, and all morality, instead of constituting them on a new basis; it therefore acts in contradiction to all past historical experience.*[776-779] *The Communist revolution is the most radical rupture with traditional property relations...and traditional ideas.*[791-794]

Marx insists that the Communist ideology is totally new; in reality, Communism is simply humanity at its lowest ebb, appealing to the lowest common denominators of depravity. There was nothing new about that, and interim history has proven that repeatedly as it continues into the 21st Century.

[795-855]These are the final lines of Section II of Manifesto. They are repetitious, but summarize the salient points of Communism. Marx reiterates his position, and it is instructive to analyze that position, line by line exposing Communism for the great hypocrisy that it is.

Marx' teaching method is not open to discussion as he arrogantly shrugs off the nay-sayers.[795] He promises the proletariat that they will very soon rule over their oppressors, reversing the roles so that the factories and farms will become models of production. Of course, the bourgeoisie will not simply hand over the keys to the factories, so they must be taken through violence.[797-806]

Let's pause and use Marx against himself. Early on in *Manifesto* we heard Marx lament the loss of the trade guilds to the factories and to the dehumanizing effects of free trade. He castigated the globalization and overproduction caused by loss of control over market forces. Now, Marx wants to overthrow the system of overproduction and replace it by "increase[-ing] the total productive forces as rapidly as possible."

It is not immediately obvious in the text why this increase in production is so important. Is it just to create busy work for the proletariat? Is it to drive down global prices for goods and services, to destabilize American manufacturing? Whatever the case, Lenin, Stalin, and Mao took Marx' words as immutable and followed the ideology to the extreme. What they got in return was extreme confusion, extreme poverty and starvation, and ultimately – extreme control. Communists create havoc in the present so that they can repudiate the past and impose their own future. That is why they agitate (*via* "community organizers").

Marx does give a hint to the chaos.[805-812] He admits to the inevitable economic collapse, but uses it as a pretext to gain the revolution.

In a rational world one would think that after several generations of following the *Manifesto* recipe the principles would either be proven and universally acknowledged as superior, or they would be disproven and abandoned as a failed economic system.

What we have, of course, is that Communism as an economic system is an abject failure, not abandoned but eagerly adopted through threats and intimidation, sometimes open, sometimes hidden under the guise of "transformation." Free peoples of the world, beware!

[813-837]The Ten Measures* of "despotic inroads"[806] admitted by Marx' own words to be "economically insufficient and untenable"[807-808] are listed here and while tedious, it is enlightening to endure the tedium.

1. Abolition of property in land and application of all rents of land to public purposes.
2. A heavy progressive or graduated income tax.
3. Abolition of all rights of inheritance.
4. Confiscation of the property of emigrants and rebels. (Note the 'e' in emigrant)

5. Centralization of credit in the hands of the State, by means of a national bank with State capital and an exclusive monopoly.

6. Centralization of the means of communication and transport in the hands of the State.

7. Extension of factories and instruments of production owned by the State; the bringing into cultivation of waste-lands, and the improvement of the soil generally in accordance with a common plan.

8. Equal liability of all to work. Establishment of industrial armies, especially for agriculture.

9. Combination of agriculture with manufacturing industries; gradual abolition of all the distinction between town and country by a more equable distribution of the population over the country.

10. Free education for all children in public schools. Abolition of children's factory labor in its present form. Combination of education with industrial production, &c., &c.

*The Ten Measures is an unmistakable allusion to the Biblical Ten Commandments.

Clearly, some of this is good. Education, child labor laws, the right to work, agriculture, and manufacturing are all important parts of a civil and prosperous society. However, history has shown that in practice, Communists distort all of this to their nefarious ends. Never forget that "Communism abolishes eternal truths… morality… religion"[775-778] and recreates them in its own image.

The State takes ownership and control over all private property, so no one will have a home to call their own or to do with as they please. There is no freedom of the press, nor will any citizen be allowed to travel without State permission.

State banking will control all money (think Euros!); anyone with money will lose it through taxes and won't even be able to give their children an inheritance, which will be illegal. Arguing with the State or escaping the country won't help either, as all your possessions will be stolen.

Government will control all manufacturing and farming, and will decide who does what and where they do it. If moving farmers onto collectives seems like a fine idea, that is exactly what will be done (and so it happened in Russia and China, resulting in mass starvation).

Finally, the *coup de grace* – brainwash the population. Place commissars in factories so that workers are always watched and to ensure that the political messages never cease. Schools are places of indoctrination so that children will know who is really in control (hint: it is not their parents). Accomplish that and a Communist country is radicalized in one generation. Brilliant!

[839]"When, in the course of development, class distinctions disappear…" (Sound familiar? The US Declaration of Independence begins in similar fashion: "When in the course of human Events, it becomes necessary for one People…").

"When all production has been concentrated in the hands of a vast association of the whole nation…"[839-842] is a misrepresentation of great semantic proportion. One of the promises of Communism is to take all the property and factories and redistribute them, placing control in the hands of the proletariat which *would* be vast. However, the word *concentrated* defies *vast*. Things are concentrated so that they can occupy limited spaces. Therefore, the concentrated power of a vast empire (whether of manufacturing or people) must be placed in the hands of individuals or other very small cadre. Otherwise, the power will dilute and no longer be powerful.

Marx goes on[842-855] to fantasize about the coming utopian society, which he again calls an "association", and predicts "free development of all". Unfortunately for the billions to live under the shackles of Communism, human nature will define a very different course.

[858-1227]Socialist and Communist literature.

In this section, Marx diverts from his diatribe to describe the Socialist condition of 19th Century Europe. "Feudal Socialism"[861-917] describes flailing French and English aristocrats trying desperately to hold on to the past while placating the future. Their royal power slipping away, they tried to double dip – keeping their wealth and privilege while portraying themselves as the champions of the new proletariat (eerily familiar in modern American politics!).

"Petty*-Bourgeois Socialism"[919-969] If the aristocracy stooped to the proletariat, the Petty-Bourgeois aspired towards it. Marx agreed with these writers so long as they used their pens against big business, acquisition of capital, and "the crying inequalities in the distribution of wealth".[954-955] (Interestingly, these writers correctly predicted the coming world wars and the breakdown of morality and national identity[955-957]).

*"*Petty*" is more accurately written as "*Petite*" but is found both ways in literature.

Marx disagreed and ultimately dismissed the petty bourgeois because they would eventually allow some of the old property relations to emerge (this concept was considered to be "reactionary", [964]thus a deviation from pure Communist ideology).

German or "True" Socialism.[971-1077] Marx had a habit of belittling his literati kin. Of course, as a traitor to Germany he could hardly give them credit for advancing *his* cause. Marx consigned the German Socialists to the trash heap under the guise of being reactionary.[1047] Marxism is the only pure Communist ideology; all others are pretenders to the throne, and must be swept away.[1052-1077] Dialogue is an abomination to Communism.

Conservative or Bourgeois Socialism.[1080-1126] In the Marxist worldview, there is no room for any other philosophy, thought, ideology, or construct that promotes social change without extreme violence, eradication of all social norms, and annihilation of the old order. "The bourgeois is a bourgeois – for the benefit of the working class".[1125-1126]

Conservatives were no different from reactionaries, in that they did not draw clear lines of demarcation between proletariat and bourgeois; thus, their denunciation. (The 20th Century Communist leaders would take this to the extremes of paranoia, eradicating all posers, real or imagined, to keep themselves in power. 100,000,000 lives later….).

Critical-Utopian Socialism and Communism.[1128-1227] This era predated *Manifesto*, and did not make class distinction clear enough for Marx, who stepped over and discarded them as infantile. [1147-1151] Furthermore, Utopians made two cardinal errors:

- Utopians "want to improve the condition of every member of society, even that of the most favored"; [1169-1171] and,
- "They wish to attain their ends by peaceful means, necessarily doomed to failure". [1178-1181]

We have seen repeatedly that Marxist Communism seeks the utter destruction of its enemies, and that through violence and social upheaval; anything less is unacceptable. Marx designates the Utopians not as allies (in Communism there is no such thing as "loyal opposition"), but as "reactionary conservative Socialists". [1219]

IV. Position of the Communists in Relation to the Various Existing Opposition Parties [1229-1286] This is the Grand Finale that was not to be, at least not in Marx' time. Marx called for immediate action around the globe, [1235, 1271-1273] particularly in Germany. [1263] Marx must have had some scores to settle in his home country and, like many Communists, he wanted a call to arms for others to do his dirty work. The revolution in Germany sputtered and died, and it would take a half century for the real revolution to begin, in Russia. Lenin and Stalin would be Marx' minions, taking the Manifesto and growing it to staggering proportions.

Marx' vision of the future may have been that of a prairie fire sweeping the horizon, consuming everything in its path, stopping only when rage had devoured all the fuel and air and created a vacuum into which he would walk, triumphant.

Perhaps he saw the future as a global catastrophe, a giant earthquake that brings down once mighty structures over the heads of all living creatures. The cries of the wounded would stir no pity in his cruel soul, not one twinge of regret. Marx would not reach out with the hands of a compassionate healer. Nay! His mighty fists would search the rubble of broken humanity until he found not their hearts, but their throats, and squeeze until they breathed their last.[1279-1284]

Working Men of All Countries, Unite!

***

Marx' zeal for world domination never flagged. He died in 1883 unfulfilled in life, a pathetic, narcissistic, predatory alcoholic, evil to the end. One can only imagine the horrible dungeons of the Hell where he is confined, and wonder if he, Karl Marx, ever repented…

Father Abraham, have pity on me!
Send Lazarus to dip the tip of his finger in water and
cool my tongue, Because I am in agony in this fire.

Luke 16:24

Final words

As of March 2018, according to the internet, there are only five Communist countries: China, Cuba, Laos, North Korea, and Vietnam. Many authors and journalists would also consider Russia to be unofficially so, and would rope in Venezuela and Nicaragua due to their actions in recent decades. There are also many other countries with Communist political parties.

Interestingly, the US Navy sent an aircraft carrier to Vietnam on a peaceful mission just this month! This event is interpreted as a move to support Vietnam against threats from China...hmm-m-m. According to Marx, mature Communist countries should be very friendly towards each other, and such antagonisms should be dissolving.

America so far is not Communist. By "so far" I mean that we as a nation are moving rapidly toward becoming a totalitarian state. There is no doubt that radical groups are agitating neighborhoods and cities such as Ferguson, MO, and Baltimore, MD. This is a frightening trend, and it needs to be reversed if we are to keep America free.

I will keep writing and educating. How about you – will you fight to keep your birthright?

Author Biography

Don Wolfram is a happily married father of three extraordinary kids. Before that he was a Marine, a world traveler, and a *faux* mountain man in the Montana wilderness. He eventually came to his senses and returned to Kansas to pursue higher education and make himself useful to society.

Don and his wife Roxanne are fully committed to raising great kids into great adults and world changers through Jesus. They share the joys and burdens of parenting with friends and family. Don works as a family physician when he is not somewhere with his head buried in a book.